SDIYOLAR
PROJECTS UPDATED EDITION

SMALL PROJECTS TO WHOLE-HOME SYSTEMS:
TAP INTO THE SUN

ERIC SMITH
and
PHILIP SCHMIDT
with
TROY WANEK

COOL
SPRINGS
PRESS
Home and Garden Experts

MINNEAPOLIS, MINNESOTA

Quarto is the authority on a wide range of topics.

Quarto educates, entertains and enriches the lives of our readers—enthusiasts and lovers of hands-on living.

www.quartoknows.com

First published in 2017 by Cool Springs Press, an imprint of Quarto Publishing Group USA Inc., 400 First Avenue North, Suite 400, Minneapolis, MN 55401 USA. Telephone: (612) 344-8100
Fax: (612) 344-8692

quartoknows.com
Visit our blogs at quartoknows.com

Cool Springs Press titles are also available at discounts in bulk quantity for industrial or sales-promotional use. For details contact the Special Sales Manager at Quarto Publishing Group USA Inc., 400 First Avenue North, Suite 400, Minneapolis, MN 55401 USA.

10 9 8 7 6 5 4 3 2 1

ISBN: 978-1-59186-664-0

Library of Congress Cataloging-in-Publication Data

Names: Smith, Eric W. (Eric William), 1951- author.
Title: DIY solar projects : small projects to whole-home systems : tap into the sun / Eric Smith.
Other titles: Solar projects | Do it yourself solar projects
Description: Updated edition. | Minneapolis, Minnesota : Quarto Publishing Group USA Inc., Cool Springs Press, 2016. | Includes index.
Identifiers: LCCN 2016034412 | ISBN 9781591866640 (pbk.)
Subjects: LCSH: Solar houses--Amateurs' manuals. | Dwellings--Energy conservation--Amateurs' manuals. | Photovoltaic power generation--Amateurs' manuals. | Solar heating--Amateurs' manuals.
Classification: LCC TH7414 .S63 2016 | DDC 644--dc23
LC record available at https://lccn.loc.gov/2016034412

Acquiring Editor: Mark Johanson
Authors: Eric Smith and Philip Schmidt
Edition Editor: Troy Wanek
Project Manager: Jordan Wiklund
Art Director: Brad Springer
Cover Designer: Jay Smith–Juicebox Designs
Layout: Danielle Smith-Boldt

On the front cover: Installation of a rooftop solar panel.

On the back cover: Solar oven (left); portable solar cart (middle); solar thermal collector (right).

Printed in China

MIX
Paper from responsible sources
FSC® C101537

NOTICE TO READERS

S ● LAR PROJECTS
DIY
UPDATED EDITION

Contents

INTRODUCTION

It's difficult to overstate the value of solar energy on Earth. The sun is by far the most plentiful, accessible, and reliable source of renewable energy, or energy period. It provides more power—in the forms of heat and light (and with light, electricity)—than we could ever use. And not only is solar energy infinitely abundant, it's absolutely free and available to everyone. You don't have to dig for it, and you can't own it, dam it, go to war over it, charge for it, or turn it off.

So why haven't we done more with solar energy? That's a very good question, especially when you consider how easy it can be to harness the sun's power. You do it every day, in fact. Opening the shades on a winter morning to let sunlight into a room captures solar radiation. The same effect helps to dry clothes on a clothesline. It's not just warmed air that heats the room or dries the clothes; the sunlight itself contains heat energy that warms anything it touches. That's how the sun can heat the interior of your home (which works like a greenhouse) when it's well below zero outside.

The same principle makes all solar heating possible and is the basis of many solar-powered devices—from solar ovens and water purifiers to lumber kilns and water heating systems. All of these make great DIY projects that not only teach you about solar energy; they'll actually save you some money and reduce your use of non-renewable fuels. And all you have to do is let in the sun.

The other primary application of solar energy is, of course, electricity. While not as simple as capturing solar heat, turning sunlight into usable power has become as easy as choosing a plug-and-play system and setting it up wherever the sun is shining. Solar power equipment has entered a new age of availability and affordability, and you can now buy solar panels, batteries, and other essentials online from the same places you might order books or razor refills (they might even ship in the same package!).

Granted, powering a household with solar electricity isn't something you can accomplish in a weekend (or without professional help), but learning the basics of photovoltaics (PV) gives you an understanding of solar electric systems of all types and sizes, from battery trickle-chargers to RV and boat power to large home systems that can roll back your utility meter or free you from the power grid entirely.

This book provides a quick and easy education on the science behind solar heat and electricity, teaching you just what you need to know to get started on your own solar projects…and that's where the fun starts. You'll learn how to build your own equipment for cooking food, heating your house, heating and purifying water, and even drying lumber with the sun. On the electrical side of things, you'll learn all about small, DIY-friendly off-grid systems as well as how to plan for large-scale home installations. For power on the go, there's help with choosing systems and components for RVs, boats, and other mobile applications.

No matter which projects you choose, the sun will be waiting to bring it to life.

Wherever the Sun Shines...

You may have heard something like this before: every hour, the sun delivers enough energy to the earth to meet global energy demands for an entire year. This gives you a general sense of the enormity of solar potential, but it might help to consider the same idea on a more human scale: a single square meter of direct sunlight provides 1,000 watts of energy. Capturing that same amount of light in a solar panel can produce about 170 watts of usable electricity—enough to power over a dozen energy-efficient light bulbs or even a big-screen TV. A homemade solar cooker can use a meter of light to boil a pot of water in a few minutes, and a simple hot air collector can employ it to heat a small room or warm up a garage.

As these simple examples demonstrate, solar systems don't have to be big or expensive to be effective, and you can accomplish a lot of different things with a small amount of sunlight. Here's a look at just a few of the many practical—and doable—ways to put your own patch of sunlight to work, whether you're in the house, out in the backyard, deep in the woods, or on the road.

Solar collectors and heaters are ideal for sheds, cabins, and other outbuildings that get a lot of daytime use. This remote log cabin sports a simple collector that generates enough electricity to power a couple of lights and a radio.

Hot-air collectors for space heating are DIY-friendly and great for experimentation. A basic design starts with a wood or metal box that gets painted black and filled with any material that can collect heat and create airflow, such as metal ducting, dryer vent hose, or even soda cans.

Roof not right for solar? No problem. Ground-mounting solves all sorts of logistical (and aesthetic) issues for both PV and solar thermal systems. Mounting racks can be purchased or built from scratch.

Rooftop solar isn't just for houses. Standard rigid solar panels (still the best all-around type of panel) work well on boats, RVs, trailers, and other vehicles.

Purify and filter water: A solar still (left) works just fine to distill and purify water for modest consumption. A solar-powered pump (right) also may be used to filter water in off-the-grid locales.

Heat fast, cook slow: A dish-type or parabolic solar cooker (left) creates a focused point of intense heat that can ignite paper in a matter of seconds or, more usefully, heat water or cook food relatively quickly. Cooking in a heat-trapping solar oven (right) is an all-day affair, but even homemade units can reach temperatures upwards of 300°F.

12-volt off-grid power systems are ideal for DIYers getting into solar electricity. Virtually the same system can supply permanent power to a shed or cabin, RV, camper, or boat to provide "house" power without help from an engine or generator (top), or be mounted on a wagon or trailer for portable power (bottom).

Solar water heating systems can heat water for domestic use (drinking, showering, etc.) or for water-based space heating systems. In both cases, the solar system typically preheats the water and a conventional water heater or boiler takes it from there. Commercial hot-water systems (top) save fuel, although the cost savings vary. DIY systems (bottom) can offer better payback potential.

Solar garages and carports can shelter and recharge electric vehicles at the same time. Excess power can be put to use elsewhere on the property, for outdoor lighting and outlets or even to provide supplemental power to a building.

Combining solar thermal and PV systems once seemed like the ultimate way to go solar, but declining costs for solar electricity have made thermal systems hard to justify in many cases. It's often more cost-efficient to install a larger PV system and have it supply an electric resistance or heat pump water heater than to install a new thermal system for domestic hot water.

SOLAR ELECTRICITY

When NASA scientists of the 1950s needed a revolutionary source of power for their spacecraft, they had to look and think beyond the Earth. Their challenge was monumental, yet their solution poetically simple: They would find a way to tap into the most abundant, most accessible, and most reliable source of energy in the solar system—the sun.

The science of solar power is known as photovoltaics, or PV, which describes the basic process of changing sunlight into electricity. PV systems are incredibly versatile and are used to power everything from cell phone chargers to houses to entire cities. The economic benefits of PV can be significant, and when you consider that supplying the average home with conventional power creates over three tons of carbon emissions each year (over twice that of the average car), the environmental benefits of pollution-free solar electricity are nothing to squint at.

This chapter introduces you to the most popular solar options for supplementing your existing systems or even declaring energy independence with an "off-grid" home. As solar technology continues its journey from the space program to suburban rooftops and beyond, anyone serious about climbing aboard will find a vibrant marketplace that's more than ready to help.

IN THIS CHAPTER:

- How Sunlight Becomes Electricity
- Solar Power Basics
- Mounting Solar Modules
- Solar Electricity Safety
- Installing Simple DC Systems
- 12-Volt Solar Light System
- Solar-Powered Security Light
- Planning for Whole-House Power
- Mobile Solar: RVs, Boats & Portable Power

With every passing year, solar panels become more efficient and less expensive. The day when a solar panel array is installed on every roof to provide power for the home and for the larger electrical grid may not be too far off.

How Sunlight Becomes Electricity

Individual units of solar energy, called photons, are absorbed by the solar cells, which contain a negative (n-type) and positive (p-type) layer of silicon. The photons cause electrons to move toward the negative conductor of the circuit, leaving behind a space, or "hole." This causes an electron to move into the hole, leaving a hole in its own place. The process is continuous as electrons are returned to the module from the circuit to fill in the holes at the same rate as other electrons leave the module, creating a flow of electricity.

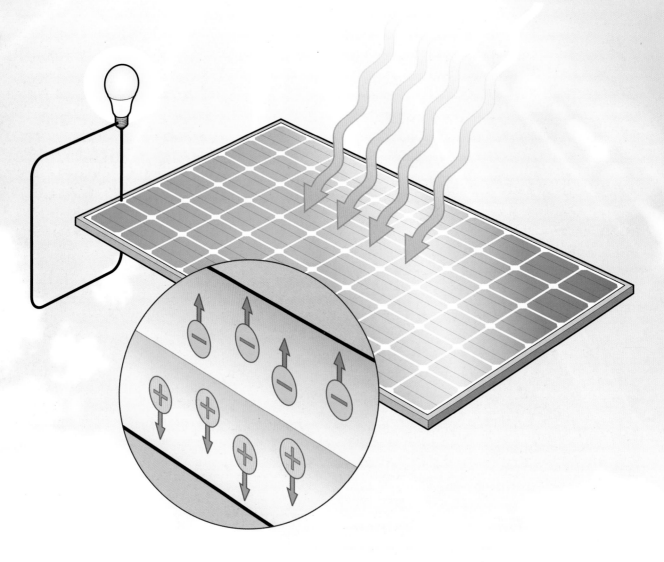

Solar Power Basics

Here's how PV power works: A solar panel—or more properly, solar module—is made up of solar cells, each containing thin layers of silicon, the same material used widely in the computer industry. Silicon has semi-conductive properties. Sunlight is absorbed by the cells in the module, initiating an electron exchange between the layers of silicon to produce electrical power. Connecting the module with wires creates an electrical circuit and a means for harnessing this electrical activity. Solar modules can be installed in a series to create a solar "array." The size of an array, as well as the quality of the modules' semiconductor material, determines its power output.

The electricity produced by solar cells is DC, or direct current, which is what most batteries produce (and what battery-powered devices run on). Household electrical systems and standard appliances run on AC, or alternating current, electricity. Powering these items requires an inverter that converts the DC power from the modules (or batteries) to AC power. It's all the same to your appliances, and they run just as well on solar-generated power as on standard utility power.

Converting from DC to AC isn't always necessary or ideal. Many small PV systems, such as those supplying a workshop or greenhouse, as well as portable systems used on boats and recreational vehicles, are set up for DC power and include DC appliances and devices. Even some household systems employ highly efficient DC appliances that don't require conversion. Considerations and options for using AC versus DC power are discussed throughout this chapter.

Solar Module Design

PV modules come in a range of types for different applications and power needs. The workhorse of the group is the glass- or plastic-covered rigid panel that can be installed on the roof or wall of a house or other structure, on the ground, or on special mounts for mobile and marine applications. Panel arrays can also be mounted onto solar-powered tracking systems that follow the sun for increased productivity.

Rigid modules, sometimes called framed modules, are designed to withstand all types of weather, including hail, snow, and extreme winds; manufacturers typically offer warranties of 20 to 25 years, but modules are designed to last much longer.

Small modules come in almost any size, while larger units typically are 1 meter wide, following a worldwide standard. Roughly speaking, the larger the panel the more power it produces. On a standard rigid panel, each 6 × 6-inch cell outputs about 0.5 volts at about 8 amps. That translates to 4 watts of power (volts × amps = watts). A small panel used to charge a single battery might produce 10 to 30 watts of power, while a large panel for a household system might be rated at 250 or 300 watts (see Module Ratings and Efficiency, on page 19).

In addition to variations in size, shape, wattage rating and other specifications, standard PV modules can be made with two different types of silicon cells. Monocrystalline cells contain a higher grade of silicon and typically offer about 3 percent higher efficiency (see Module Ratings and Efficiency, on page 19) than polycrystalline cells. Monocrystalline units typically cost a bit more, but warranties on panels often are comparable.

Photovoltaic cells made from polycrystalline silicon (top) often have square corners, and the cell structure has a visibly flaky appearance. Monocrystalline cells (bottom) often have rounded corners. Square cells have a greater surface area, which can help polycrystalline modules offer similar output to monocrystalline modules despite a lower cell efficiency.

POLYCRYSTALLINE

MONOCRYSTALLINE

Anatomy of a Solar Module

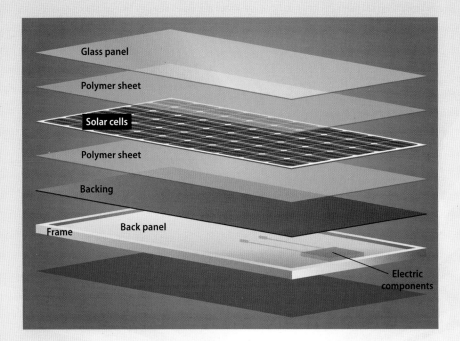

Glass panel

Polymer sheet

Solar cells

Polymer sheet

Backing

Frame   **Back panel**

Electric components

Solar modules are relatively simple pieces of equipment. They are housed within a metal frame, usually aluminum, that frames a back panel to which the electric components are attached. A rigid backing material is at the bottom of the configuration. The solar cells are sandwiched between two polymer sheets that are bonded to the backing. The layers are protected with a glass panel on top that is held in place by the frame.

Module Ratings & Efficiency

Solar modules carry STC (Standard Test Conditions) ratings for voltage output, wattage, and other performance criteria. STC ratings typically appear on a manufacturer's nameplate or label on the back of the module itself. Common ratings include:

P_{mp}: Power maximum power—the maximum wattage output of a module under STC. The "nameplate" or working watts of the module at STC. Calculated by multiplying $V_{mp} \times I_{mp}$: $V_{mp} \times I_{mp} = P_{mp}$.

Voc: Open-circuit voltage—the maximum voltage output when the module is not connected to a load or system component). This is the highest potential voltage at STC, but it can go significantly higher in cold temperatures. This value is primarily for electrical safety considerations and evaluating equipment compatibility.

V_{mp}: Volts maximum power—voltage output when the module is connected to a load; this is the maximum voltage produced when the module is connected to

a working system and is used to calculate power and energy production.

I_{mp}: Current maximum power—amperage when the module is connected to a load and is the working current, used in power and energy calculations.

Isc: Short-circuit current—amperage when the module wires are connected or shorted out. Calculated as the worst-case scenario for wire sizing at STC.

The *efficiency* of a solar module refers to how effectively the unit converts sunlight to electricity. A new monocrystalline module may have an efficiency of about 17 percent STC. That means that 17 percent of the sunlight that hits the panel is converted to DC electricity. For example, a 1.5 × 1.5-meter module rated at 250 watts power tilted perpendicularly to the noon sun would be 16.6 percent efficient:

250 watts output ÷ 1500 watts sunlight input
(STC = 1,000 watts/square meter) = 16.6%

It's important to note that efficiency, like STC ratings, is calculated under laboratory (ideal) conditions. The actual efficiency of a working module is reduced by several factors, including sunlight intensity, shade, temperature, and the age of the panel. Solar cells are less efficient in hot weather, and they gradually degrade over time. Due to this degradation, module manufacturers typically guarantee efficiency on a sliding scale. It's common for a warrantee to stipulate a minimum of 80 percent of the rated efficiency after 25 years.

It's also important to note that efficiency with PV systems is different from that of other energy-converting systems, such as a furnace or air conditioner. With a furnace, for example, efficiency tells you how much usable heat you get for the amount of energy source (gas, propane, electricity, etc.) consumed. You're paying for the gas, and any gas that's not converted to usable heat is considered waste. With a solar system, the energy source—sunlight—is completely free, and nothing is really consumed, so conventional notions of waste don't apply.

Efficiency of a solar module may not relate to energy savings, but it does relate to size. A more efficient module creates more electricity for its size than a less efficient module and offers the advantage of occupying less area on your rooftop or other location where space may be scarce. However, higher efficiency comes with a higher price tag, and because you're not paying for the energy source, efficiency doesn't translate to quicker payback. In other words, a slightly larger array of cheaper, less efficient modules might be a better investment than a smaller array of higher-efficiency units—provided you have the space for the larger array and the modules are of good quality from a reputable manufacturer.

A typical 100-watt solar module is around 26 × 42" in size. More efficient modules can deliver the same amount of wattage but in a smaller footprint.

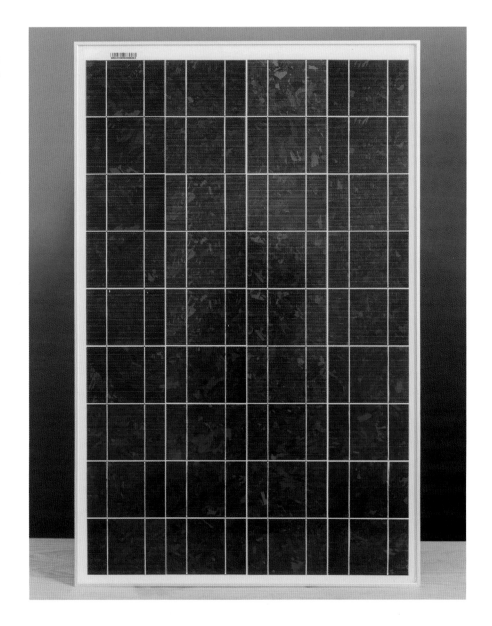

PV Systems At a Glance

Solar electric power is fascinating, exciting, and, for many people, pretty confusing. A solar module wired directly to an attic fan or water pump makes sense: the DC electricity produced by the module directly powers the fan or pump, running it only when the sun is out. But as solar systems get bigger and more complex, you may need fuses, charge controllers, inverters, system monitors, and other components, all of which must be compatible and installed properly for the system to operate safely and efficiently.

This extra equipment is required whenever solar modules are used to store power in batteries, send power to a house or other structure, or tie into the utility grid. To help visualize how different systems work and the components required, we've assembled a series of sample systems, starting with a basic module powering a fan and continuing up to a large, whole-house power system.

Most of the pieces are easy to understand once you know what they do, and you don't have to be an electrical engineer to design a basic system. If you need help with choosing components and assembling a simple setup, many solar equipment suppliers offer technical support to make sure you have everything you need. For any system that's attached to your house or is intended to power more than a small device or two, you must also consult the local building department. Most building authorities require a permit for systems with a system voltage of more than 50 volts.

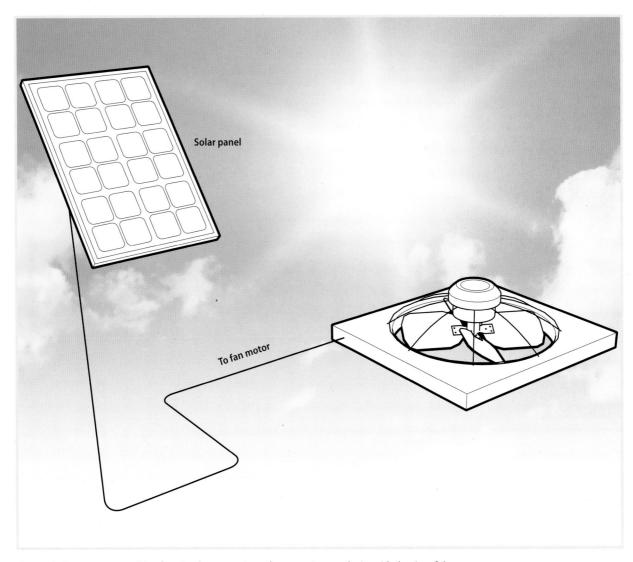

Solar panel

To fan motor

Photovoltaic systems start with a few simple connections, then grow in complexity with the size of the array.

A Starter System with Low-Watt Panel

In this type of low-wattage system power flows directly from the solar module to a DC motor, light, roof fan, or battery. When the sun is out, the device works; as the sun goes down, the device slows down and finally stops. A low-wattage module like this (less than 5 watts) can also be used to top off a 12V battery or keep a battery that's in storage charged during the winter, because the amount of power generated is low enough that there's no danger of overcharging.

Solar-powered garden lights are slightly more sophisticated because the module charges a small rechargeable battery during the day instead of powering the light directly. The battery then powers the light when it gets dark.

Cell phone chargers are small and lightweight, and generally produce 5 watts or less of power. A basic solar module such as this doesn't store power—it will only charge the cell phone when the sun is out.

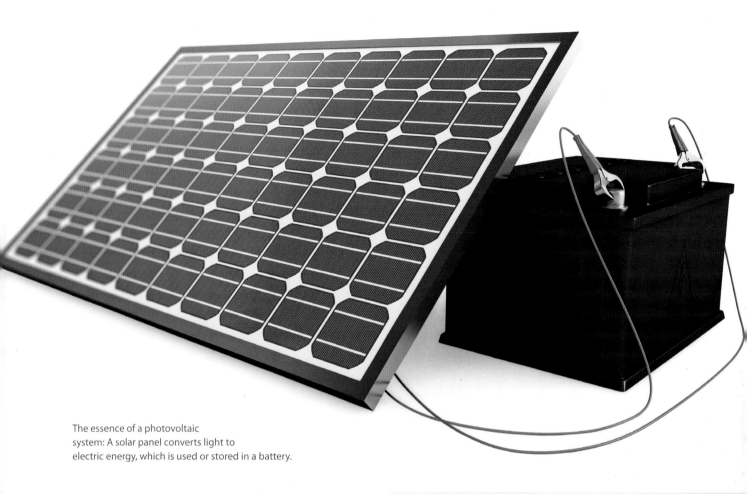

The essence of a photovoltaic system: A solar panel converts light to electric energy, which is used or stored in a battery.

A solar drip charger is connected to the terminals of a car, RV, or boat battery to keep it fully charged when it is not in use for extended periods of time.

Portable, foldable solar panels are small enough to fit in a backpack or pocket, but have enough power to keep electronic gizmos charged up. You can even plug one into your car's cigarette lighter to top off the battery.

More Watts Equals More Work

As with the starter system, the DC motor in the pump used to refill this stock tank is powered directly by the solar panel, with no battery, and will not operate unless the sun is out. However, when the sun is out, the pump will operate more efficiently and produce more water than it would if the solar energy flowed through a battery, because up to a quarter of the energy generated by a solar panel can be lost when it is stored in a battery. The pump is given another boost by a linear current booster, which provides extra power to the pump when the light is low.

This type of system needs a larger panel to operate—typically 50 to 60 watts or more—and is usually sized by the solar panel dealer based on the well depth, pump size, and other factors. It's the perfect system for the stock tank; the supply of water stockpiled in the tank on sunny days is more than enough for the demand, so no battery is needed. Roof vent fans, and pond pumps for water circulation and small fountains, are other types of solar-powered fixtures that use power directly from the PV panels without a battery because they don't need to run at night.

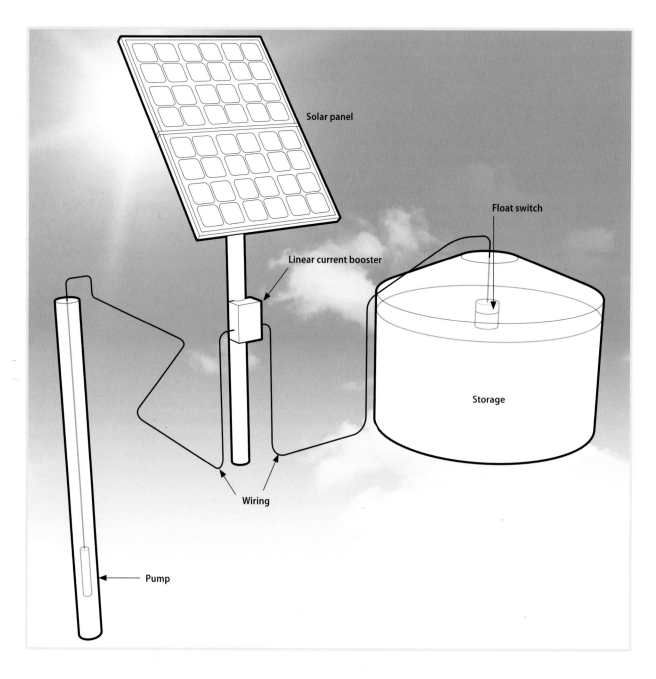

Solar panel

Float switch

Linear current booster

Storage

Wiring

Pump

Once powered by a windmill that needed frequent maintenance, this deep well, which pumps water to a nearby stock tank, is now powered directly by solar modules. Instead of pumping on demand, the motor pumps water continuously when the sun is out and stores it in a large tank.

Water for irrigation is continuously pumped from a deep aquifer up to this storage tank during the day as long as the sun is shining.

A solar-powered roof vent fan draws hot air from the attic during the day when the sun is out—the time when the attic is hottest. This type of fan generally does not include a battery, and is powered directly by the solar module (although some manufacturers offer models with backup wind or AC power).

A multimeter is a good diagnostic tool for checking a photovoltaic module to ensure it is working properly. It also allows you to check the power generated at different angles and locations.

Portable Power

This type of system begins to look more familiar, with a storage battery and a few AC outlets that can be used to power small appliances, electronics, lights, and even power tools. "Plug-and-play" type systems are generally under 100 watts, and are often small enough to be portable. Think of them as a silent alternative to a small gas-powered generator. They're useful for camping, emergency power, recreation, powering small garages and utility buildings, and similar uses. You can find pre-packaged systems at suppliers, or you can assemble your own from the individual components. In this system several pieces of electrical equipment are added between the solar panel and the devices using the power:

- **Charge controller.** A charge controller regulates the amount of power going into the battery, and prevents the battery from being overcharged.
- **12V battery.** The battery stores energy collected when the sun is out, making power available at night.
- **Inverter.** The inverter converts DC power coming from the battery into AC power, which is what most appliances and electronics use. Although DC appliances and lights are available, the selection is limited and

often more expensive. However, DC appliances and lights don't require the inverter.
- **Small catastrophe fuse.** A small-capacity fuse is a safety feature, and is placed on the positive wire between the battery and the PV panel.

A simple solar power system makes life in a yurt much easier. Inside the yurt a battery provides electricity for a few small appliances and a light.

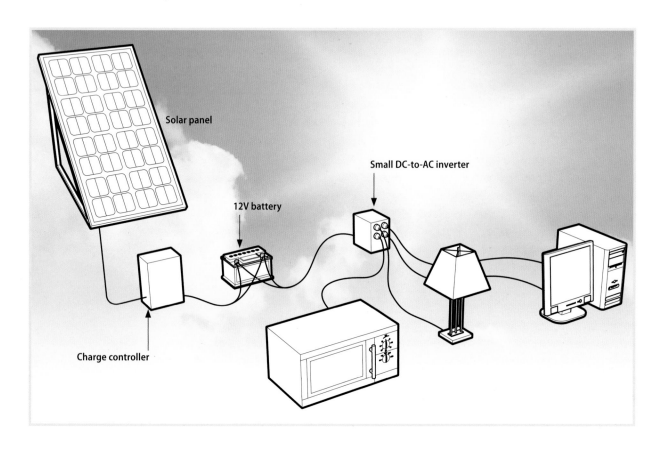

Solar panel

12V battery

Small DC-to-AC inverter

Charge controller

Solar power road signs are a common sight on highways. The light is plugged into a battery, which stores power produced by the PV panel. A charge controller keeps the battery from overcharging.

Buoy lights are a perfect use for a solar panel and battery. No other power source comes close to working as well and as cheaply for this application.

A solar panel and a small deep-cycle battery are a cleaner, quieter, and lighter source of temporary power for a trip away from the power grid.

Off-Grid System for a Small Cabin or Weekend House

This system is large enough for a small, energy-efficient off-grid cabin or vacation home, providing power for lights, a well, electronics, and a few basic appliances. If you do the installation and wiring yourself, the components for a system such as this can be surprisingly affordable; some online dealers sell packages for $2,000 to $5,000. A small gas-powered generator or windmill can also be added to the system if needed for a backup power source during cloudy periods.

Larger houses or houses with lots of power-hungry appliances need additional solar panels and batteries, based on the size of the house, the power usage, location, and other factors. Solar panel suppliers can help you size the system, and additional panels and batteries can always be added in the future.

The additional components used in this system are:

- **DC safety disconnect.** The safety disconnect allows you to shut off the flow of power from the panels to the battery for maintenance or repairs.

A small solar array in an off-the-grid cabin can provide some minimal power for ongoing use, as well as backup power.

- **DC load center.** The DC equivalent of a circuit-breaker box.
- **AC circuit breaker.** This is a small version of the circuit-breaker box found in almost every home.
- **System monitor.** A system monitor tracks power consumption and will let you know if your batteries are getting dangerously low (fully discharging a deep-cycle battery will shorten its life).

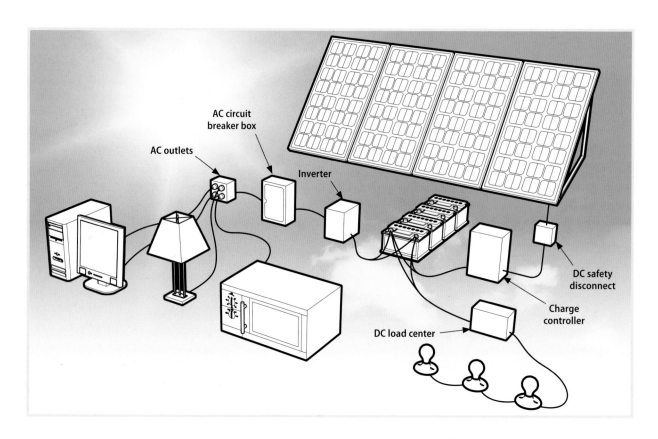

This small, energy-efficient modern house uses PV panels for power. Energy is conserved with energy-efficient appliances, extra insulation, a light-colored roof to deflect heat, and louver-shaded windows.

A camper van this size consumes as much energy as a small house, all of which would normally be generated by idling the motor. Although the large solar panels are a significant investment, they pay for themselves quickly in this desert campground, and they're also completely silent.

Whole House, Grid-Connected System

A whole-house system connected to the power grid will need an array of solar panels producing several thousand watts of power to meet household needs (depending on house size, energy efficiency, and other factors), but the system is fairly straightforward, especially if you dispense with the battery backup. Power flows to a grid-tied inverter designed to work with the utility-system electrical grid. The incoming DC power from the solar panels is converted to AC with an inverter, then it passes through a disconnect switch and a solar production meter, which tracks all solar-generated power. From there, the electricity is fed into the household's circuit-breaker box and is used just like power from the utility. Any power that's not used in the home flows into the electrical grid through a net meter, running the meter backwards. The electrical grid functions like a battery, absorbing extra power or providing it, as needed. If you create more power than you use, most utility companies will pay you or credit you for the excess.

One of the advantages of this type of system is that you can start small, then add additional solar panels later. It also eliminates the need for expensive batteries and ensures a continuous, reliable flow of power. However, if the utility company suffers a blackout, the solar panels will not be able to provide power to the house unless you have a battery backup system in place.

If your house already has power lines coming in from the utility company, it makes sense to leave them connected when you install solar panels so you can use the electrical grid for storage and backup.

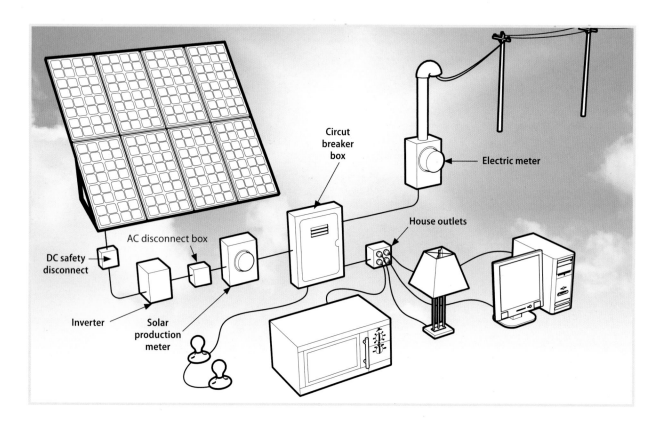

DC safety disconnect

AC disconnect box

Inverter

Solar production meter

Circut breaker box

Electric meter

House outlets

This house is still connected to the electrical grid, but with the entire south side of the roof covered with solar panels, the homeowner generates enough electricity on sunny days to earn money back from the utility company.

Power generated by wind or water supplements solar-generated power, providing an alternative source of power at night or in cloudy weather. It can also be wired to the same grid-tied system that the solar panels are connected to.

Mounting Solar Modules

Mounting an array of solar modules so everything stays in place for decades can be the most demanding part of a solar installation. With so much surface area the modules can catch gusts of wind almost as well as a sail. An array also must hold up against rain, snow loads, hail, and whatever else nature dishes out. This requires secure mounting to a roof, the ground, or the side of a house or other structure, using rust-resistant metal poles or racking and the best stainless-steel hardware.

Although home-built solar water and heat collectors can be mounted on wood posts on the ground, PV modules have a longer life expectancy and are best mounted on steel or aluminum supports that can hold up to the weather indefinitely, especially up on a roof. If the panels are roof-mounted, the condition of the roof should also be evaluated before they're installed. The panels can last well over 25 years, perhaps even 50 or more, and if the roof will need replacement in the meantime it's best to do it before installing the panels so you can avoid the expense of removing and reinstalling the panels later. Solar equipment mounted on a standing seam metal roof is a great long-term match and does not require any roof penetrations because the equipment attaches to the standing seams.

Needless to say, it's important that the modules face the sun as directly as possible and to get the maximum sun exposure—without shading—year-round. Spend some time on research and observation before you proceed with installation to avoid putting up modules that only get sufficient sun for half of the year.

Solar equipment suppliers can recommend mounting systems for the modules they sell, but the following pages will give you an overview of the standard options and considerations. If you'd like to build your own mounting rack for a single module or small array, you can adapt the project shown on pages 124–127.

The large surface area of solar panels means that they must be very securely mounted to resist the force of the wind.

Roof Mounting

Rooftop installation is the most popular option for large-scale home power systems, for several reasons. Roofs typically offer large areas of open—and unused—space that's both out of the way and usually out of sight. The elevation of the roof often eliminates or reduces shading from nearby trees. And rooftop mounting typically costs less than ground mounting because the hardware is cheaper and the installation simpler.

On a sloped roof, the tilt of the modules is generally determined by the slope of the roof, although special mounting hardware is available for increasing the tilt of modules on low-slope roofs. However, many zoning departments prohibit or restrict tilting modules upwards, especially if this tilt allows the array to extend above the roof ridge. And you can install more modules if you keep them flush or parallel to the existing roof. Mounting arrays onto flat roofs requires tilted racking systems or ballasts that have frames that hold the modules at an angle to face the sun. Many of these do not require roof penetration.

A standard mounting system on a sloped roof consists of metal brackets that mount over the shingles and are anchored into the roof framing with lag screws. Each

A system of mounting rails is attached directly to the roof framing members with lag screws.

Rooftop mounting systems are made with lightweight, corrosion-resistant metal (typically aluminum), and should last at least as long as the modules. Many mounting systems are designed to work with different brands and sizes of modules.

bracket typically is set atop a piece of metal flashing that protects the shingles and helps prevent leaks. Long metal rails attach to the brackets, keeping them several inches above the roofing. The modules are then set on top of the rails and are secured with metal clips that are bolted to the rails.

Most rooftop installations are simple and straightforward, but there are some important considerations to be aware of. The local building authority likely will have specific requirements for positioning an array, such as keeping the modules a minimum distance from the roof edges to provide

traffic paths for firefighters. Also, because they're attached to the house, rooftop arrays must include means for rapid shutdown (see page 79) required by electrical code.

Another big consideration is leakage. It's critical that manufactured flashing is installed at all lag-screw penetrations through the roofing, as well as at conduit runs for wiring. Polyurethane sealant can be used to help ensure watertightness, but this must be applied according to the flashing manufacturer's (and roofing material manufacturer's) specifications and warranty requirements.

Ground Mounting

With a ground-mount system, solar modules are anchored to the ground with a single pole or multiple poles, or a combination of multiple posts or poles supporting a metal racking system. The key advantages of ground mounting are that you don't occupy roof space—and never have to remove an array to replace roofing—and you can choose the ideal tilt and position of your solar array. The main disadvantage is that the array takes up space in your landscape, and it's much more visible on the ground than on the roof (but ground mounts can serve double-duty as storage areas, sheds, or chicken coops).

Pole-mounted PV arrays typically are attached to steel poles set deeply into the ground and anchored in concrete. The depth of each hole, the amount of concrete, and the size of each steel post are determined by the square footage of the array and its height above the ground.

As an example, a single 39 × 65-inch (17.6 square feet) module set 5 feet above the ground should be mounted on

Mounting poles offer several advantages, but you must be sure that the poles are securely anchored in concrete and that the pole base is buried sufficiently deep.

To protect against damage due to frost heave and ground movement, solar arrays must be set on poles that go down below the frost line. Some handy DIYers opt to use lumber for ground-mounting. Wood structures should be built with pressure-treated lumber and must be approved by the local building authority.

a 2-inch Schedule 40 steel pole (sold at home centers) and set into the ground at least 3 feet (or below the frost line in your area) in a 12"-diameter hole filled with concrete.

When mounting an array of multiple modules it's standard to bury the poles the same distance as the above-ground height. An array that is 5 feet above the ground will have a pole or poles buried 5 feet into the ground and set in concrete. The pole size also increases. An array with four full-size modules (say, 70 square feet total area) requires a 4"-diameter pole. Ground-mount systems with multiple poles must have the poles buried below the frost line and set in concrete. Most equipment manufacturers provide design guidelines and in most cases the inspecting authority will require a letter from a structural engineer ensuring the design is appropriate for your location. An engineer letter may cost only about $250, provided you gather all of the necessary paperwork.

Modules and arrays also may be mounted to the side of a house, but they must be securely fastened to the studs with galvanized lag bolts. Mounting to the side of an aluminum- or vinyl-sided house should be a last-ditch option, though, as the large holes created by the lag bolts are difficult or impossible to repair if the collector is ever removed, unless you have pieces of the original siding.

Always select a location for the solar panel that faces south (in the northern hemisphere) and gets the maximum amount of sun hours year-round. If possible, mark the furthest extent of shadows from nearby trees and buildings during the winter, because winter shadows will be substantially longer than summer shadows, when the sun is higher overhead. Also remember to set the panel high enough so it's well above the possible snow level in the winter.

Solar Electricity Safety

Solar modules and the various components they work with have a green, environmentally friendly feeling to them that makes it easy to let down your guard and forget normal safety rules. But remember that electricity from a solar system can cause just as much damage as electricity from utility lines. Also remember that PV modules start generating electricity as soon as any light hits them, so cover the modules completely and follow manufacturer safety recommendations until the installation is complete.

First, always make sure you have all the necessary safety equipment, including safety glasses, hardhats, work gloves, and harnesses for roof work. Make sure you understand the electrical systems you're working on; if you're uncomfortable or confused, call an electrician or solar installer for help.

Any PV system that's big enough to provide power to a house or even an outbuilding needs multiple safety devices, such as grounding equipment, shutoff devices, overload protection, and circuit breakers. Full-service suppliers will provide complete systems with all the safety equipment, but if you're putting a system together on your own from discount components you bought on the internet, read up on the subject before you get started. Solar modules have metal frames and must always be grounded, whether they're on the roof or a pole in the yard.

Big metal objects outdoors can attract lightning strikes, and you need to be sure that if your array is hit, the energy will dissipate into the ground.

PV modules typically are grounded to the metal rails of their support structure with special grounding washers called WEEBs. All of the rails are grounded with a 6-gauge bare copper wire. If the modules are on the house, the grounding wire from the array is connected to a separate ground rod and bonded to the house grounding electrode system, either directly or through a grounding lug in the home's main service panel (breaker box) or a mechanical connection with the main ground wire. If the array is installed on an outbuilding or a pole away from the house, it gets a separate ground rod at that location. Ground rods typically are 8-foot-long copper-coated rods, ½"-diameter or larger, driven into the ground with just a few inches exposed. The grounding wire is attached to the rod with a ground rod clamp. Installations away from the house require a 6-gauge wire running underground back to the main house ground wire so all of the grounds are interconnected.

Check with the local building department about grounding requirements in your area. If you live in an area with frequent lightning storms, you may need to add additional grounding protection. See page 79 for other common code requirements for PV systems.

Wear a proper safety harness when working on a steep roof.

Lightning can strike anywhere, and solar panel arrays need to be properly grounded to protect them, and you, against damage.

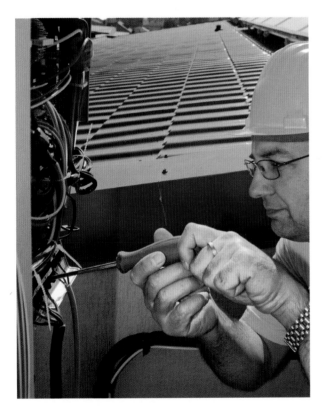

Electricity from solar panels is just as dangerous as the kind that comes over the utility lines, especially for large, whole-house arrays. The hookup to the household electrical system, as well as all connections on the AC side of the PV system, must be made by a licensed electrician.

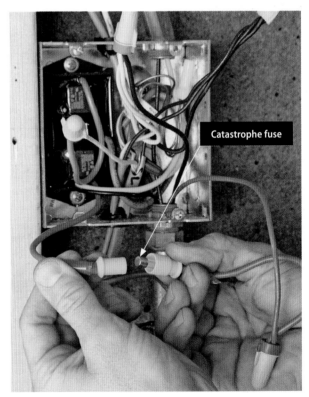

Catastrophe fuse

Remember to install all required fuses, charge controllers, and circuit breakers to ensure the safety of the system and the people using it.

Installing Simple DC Systems

The idea of powering homes with rooftop solar may be getting a lot of attention these days, but there are many other applications of solar electricity that are just as useful—and a lot more fun to experiment with. Low-voltage, DC-only systems are simple and versatile, making them ideal for DIYers getting started with solar installations. They're great for small jobs, such as powering a pond pump or keeping batteries charged up, and are just as handy for larger systems that might provide power to a garden shed or workshop, or even a solar-powered greenhouse. Solar power systems for RVs and boats also are DC-based; these and other mobile applications are discussed starting on page 81.

A basic DC system consists of a solar module, a charge controller, a battery, and wiring connections. Moving a step up in electrical capacity, a system might include multiple batteries, additional (or larger) PV modules, and components such as a DC disconnect switch or a load center, depending on the size and function of the system. DC systems can supply power directly to DC devices and appliances. If you need to plug in an AC appliance, tool, or device, simply add an AC inverter that's rated for the power draw of the AC equipment. This might be as simple as a portable car-type inverter or a larger unit that can handle several thousand watts of continuous power.

Most DC systems are 12-volt, the same voltage used by standard car and marine batteries. There are DC solar systems that run on 24 volts and higher voltages, but 12-volt systems offer some advantages for DIY projects. Namely, 12-volt systems do not require grounding. This simplifies installation and often exempts projects from permitting requirements (but it's always a good idea to have a new system inspected by an expert to make sure it's properly designed and installed). Systems that run on 24-volt and higher voltages must be grounded and typically must be permitted. Also, since 12-volt is the standard type of DC system, 12-volt-compatible products are more common than components made for higher voltages.

This section includes a discussion of battery charging and system design, followed by two sample projects that show the basic installation process for two types of 12-volt DC solar systems. These overviews give you an idea of what's involved with installing similar systems, but the specific components and steps may vary for your own project.

Battery Charging Basics

Apart from the solar module that creates the electricity, the heart of a DC system is the battery (or battery bank). That's where all of the power is drawn from: to be clear, you're never using electricity directly from the solar modules. Power always comes from the batteries. The modules' job is to recharge the batteries. The *capacity* of the batteries determines how much electricity you can use before the batteries need recharging. To increase battery capacity you can add more batteries to the system or use batteries with higher amp-hour ratings.

An amp-hour is the standard unit of measure for battery capacity, calculated by multiplying the discharge current (in amps, or amperes) by the discharge time (in hours). For example, a battery that discharges at 5 amps for 20 hours is a 100 amp-hour (Ah) battery. However, most batteries cannot be discharged completely. Lead-acid batteries, the most common type used with solar systems,

should not be discharged more than 80 percent. Draining them down more than that significantly shortens their life. Therefore, a 100 Ah battery offers—at best—only 80 amp-hours of usable power.

For maximum battery life, it's often recommended that lead-acid batteries be discharged no more than 50 percent on a regular basis. The tradeoff is that this requires a larger system to meet your needs. Discharging up to 80 percent allows for a smaller system, but the batteries won't last as long as when discharging only 50 percent with each cycle. As an example, let's say you need 200 amp-hours of power per day. If you plan to discharge up to 80 percent, increase your total battery capacity by a factor of 1.25:

200 Ah × 1.25 = 250 Ah (total capacity required)

If you plan to discharge no more than 50 percent, increase the capacity by a factor of 2:

200 Ah × 2 = 400 Ah

System Design

Designing a 12-volt power system starts with determining the battery capacity you need and then building a system that can charge the batteries in an acceptable amount of time. If you're using the power every day, the solar module or array should be capable of fully recharging the batteries in one day, based on the available sun hours at your location. If you're just keeping the batteries charged for occasional use, you can have a smaller module or array that takes more time to recharge the batteries between uses.

The primary design elements to consider are the solar module (or modules), the charge controller, and the battery (or batteries).

Module: Determine the module output based on the battery capacity and the time required for recharging the batteries. Simply put, greater output means faster recharge time. Systems may use one or more modules. If multiple, the modules may be wired in series or in parallel (see page 43), depending on the configuration.

Charge controller: Basic charge controllers with pulse width modulation (PWM) technology work fine for most systems, but charge performance is limited by the battery voltage, which varies throughout the charging cycle. When the battery voltage is low—say, 11 volts—the controller allows only 11 volts from the solar module, even if the module is producing more energy at the time. The module output must be 12 volts with PWM controllers, so multiple modules must be wired in parallel.

Better (and more expensive) charge controllers with maximum power point tracking (MPPT) technology can handle higher voltages (often 150 volts maximum, but ranging up to 600 volts with some units), allowing for full use of the available solar power. Multiple modules can be wired in series to boost the output voltage.

Three rules for choosing a charge controller:

1. Match the charge controller voltage to the battery voltage; all 12-volt systems use 12-volt controllers.
2. Match the charge controller input voltage to the solar module array voltage.
3. Choose a two-stage or three-stage controller based on the application. The three stages of charging include: 1. bulk (bringing battery to 0- to 90 percent); 2. absorption (90 to 100 percent); and 3. float (trickle-charging, keeping the battery at 100 percent). If the solar system gets occasional use but is in sunlight for long periods, a three-stage controller (which includes a float stage) is good to keep the batteries topped off.

Battery: A variety of battery types can be used for 12-volt systems, including 2-, 6-, and 12-volt batteries; see Battery Types for Solar Systems (page 46). Like solar modules, batteries can be wired in series or parallel to increase the voltage or amperage (see page 43).

Series vs. Parallel Wiring

Series and parallel are two fundamental wiring configurations used in many electrical applications. Each has advantages and disadvantages depending on the application. In 12-volt solar systems, solar modules may be wired in series or in parallel, and batteries can be wired in series, parallel, or a combination of the two. The important thing to remember is that with series wiring, the voltage increases and the amperage stays the same. With parallel wiring, the amperage increases and the voltage stays the same.

Battery series wiring: The positive of the first battery connects to the charge controller, and the negative connects to the positive of the next battery. This negative-to-positive pattern repeats until the last battery in the series; its negative connects to the charge controller. The voltage increases with each battery in the series, while the total amp-hours (or amperage output) remain the same.

Battery parallel wiring: Positives are joined to positives and negatives to negatives. The last positive and negative in the group connect to the charge controller. Voltage remains constant, while amp-hours (or amp output) are added up with each unit.

NOTE: *It is not recommended to connect more than three batteries in parallel because some of the batteries can become over- or under-utilized during charging or discharging, ultimately shortening battery life.*

Combination: This method is used to increase the voltage as well as the amp-hours of multiple batteries that are under 12 volts.

Boosting Module Voltage

Series wiring with solar modules allows you to boost the output voltage of the module array. Higher voltage reduces the effect of voltage drop, the loss of power that occurs when electricity travels along wires from one component to the next. An array that outputs at 12 volts requires relatively large wires and should be as close as possible to the batteries, to minimize the effect of voltage drop. Arrays at higher voltages can use smaller wires and be farther away from the batteries with no appreciable power loss.

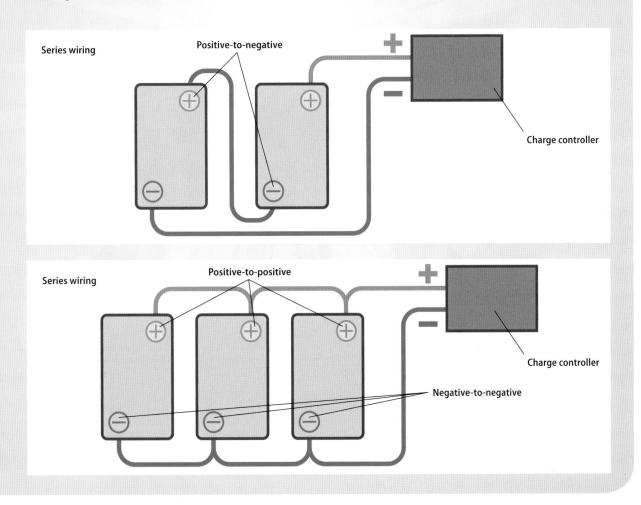

Series wiring

Positive-to-negative

Charge controller

Series wiring

Positive-to-positive

Charge controller

Negative-to-negative

Calculating Power Needs

While batteries are commonly rated in amp-hours, it's often easier to use watt-hours (Wh) when sizing a 12-volt system. To convert amp-hours to watt-hours, simply multiply by 12 (for 12 volts). A 100 Ah battery with 80 percent maximum discharge can produce 960 watt-hours with each cycle:

80 Ah × 12 volts = 960 Wh or 0.96 kWh

To estimate battery capacity needs, first add up your power needs based on your planned usage, in watt-hours (Wh). For example, if you want your DC system to power four 15-watt lights and two 60-watt fans, add up the total wattage and time of usage per day:

Lights: 60 watts @ 4 hours per day = 240 Wh

Fans: 120 watts @ 8 hours per day = 960 Wh

Total usage per day = 1,200 Wh

If you're powering any AC devices, add about 15 percent for inverter efficiency losses; see tip below.

Next, divide the watt-hours by the battery voltage to find the amp-hour requirement:

1,200 Wh ÷ 12 volts = 100 amp-hours

Then, factor in the discharge level—80 percent or 50 percent—to find the Ah rating needed to yield 100 Ah of usable energy:

100 Ahh × 1.25 = 120 Ah (80 percent discharge)

or

100 Ahh × 2 = 200 Ah (50 percent discharge)

Add Capacity for Inverters

Using an inverter with your DC system to power AC devices results in lower efficiency—typically around 85%. To account for this conversion loss, divide the watt-hour rating of the AC device by the efficiency rate:

60-watt AC device @ 8 hours per day = 960 watt-hours

960 ÷ 0.85 = 1,116 watt-hours of energy needed to operate the device

Use the higher watt-hour value for any AC devices when calculating your total battery capacity needs.

Determining Module Wattage

Once you've determined how much usable energy you need, in watt-hours or amp-hours of battery storage, you can find the module wattage required to recharge your batteries. There are four factors at play here, and the first three have already been covered:

1. Charge controller: MPPT controllers make better use of available solar energy than PWM controllers.
2. Sun hours: How much sunlight you get at your location (see page 70).
3. Derate factor: Reducing the rated module wattage by 10 percent due to lower output at high temperatures.
4. Battery efficiency: Lead-acid batteries need an additional 25 percent of input energy to recharge fully. For example, if you remove 100 watt-hours from a battery, you must recharge with 125 watt-hours to get back to the original charge.

Here's a sample calculation assuming that you need 1,200 watt-hours of battery power per day, you're buying standard 140-watt modules, and you can expect five hours of uninterrupted sunlight per day at your location:

1,200 Whh × 1.25 (battery efficiency) = 1,500 Wh to replace what was discharged

1,500 Wh ÷ 5 (daily sun hours) = 300 watts of module output

If you're using a PWM charge controller, estimate 100 watts of output from a 140-watt module:

300 W ÷ 100 W (per 140-watt module) = 3 modules*

(*must be wired in parallel for a PWM charge controller)

If you're using a MPPT charge controller, estimate with the full module wattage:

300 w ÷ 140 = 2+ modules

Choosing Modules

You can use a variety of configurations and module wattages for your 12-volt system, as shown in the chart below, and there's no single best design for every situation. One easy and common method for choosing modules is based on the fact that a 36-cell module is optimized for charging a 12-volt battery; here's why:

Modules with 36 cells produce 18 volts: 36 cells × 0.5 volt per cell = 18 volts (V_{mp}). Remember that V_{mp} is the maximum rated voltage, and the actual voltage output will be lower—down to about 15 volts when the module gets hot. A 12-volt battery needs approximately 14.7 volts to reach a full charge (which is about 12.7 volts). Therefore, even with an actual output of 15 volts, a single 36-cell (18-volt) module is just the right size to fully charge a 12-volt battery.

Using this rule, many 12-volt systems are simply designed to include one 36-cell module for each 12-volt battery, with both the modules and the batteries wired in parallel. For example, if you're using 50-amp-hour batteries, you would need:

One 50 Ah battery = One 36-cell module

Two 50 Ah batteries (wired in parallel for 100 Ah total) = Two 36-cell modules (in parallel)

Three 50 Ah batteries (150 Ah in parallel) = Three 36-cell modules (in parallel)

This simple design configuration works well for systems with one to three batteries. Since the batteries are wired in parallel, it's not advisable to use more than three batteries, due to the potential for uneven charge/discharge rates.

What's That in Watts?

Remember that watts = volts × amps. A standard 36-cell module produces about 8 amps, so the wattage rating is likely to be about 140:

18 volts × 8 amps = 144 watts

12-VOLT SYSTEM SIZING

Here are some sample design specifications for different daily energy requirements. These values apply to 1 day of energy storage and 1 day of full sun to recharge. Always perform real calculations, based on your system components and location, to ensure accuracy. It's a common mistake to underestimate recharge time, resulting in slightly undercharged batteries and premature system failure.

ENERGY USED PER DAY (WATT-HOURS)	12-VOLT BATTERY CAPACITY (AMP-HOURS)*	SOLAR ARRAY (WATTS)**	QUANTITY OF 12-VOLT (18 VMP) SOLAR MODULES WIRED IN PARALLEL
200 Wh	21 Ah	55	One 60-watt module
400 Wh	42 Ah	110	One 120-watt module or two 60-watt modules
600 Wh	63 Ah	165	Two 90-watt modules
1,200 Wh	125 Ah	330	Three 120-watt modules
1,500 Wh	156 Ah	413	Four 100-watt modules
2,000 Wh	208 Ah	550	Four 140-watt modules
2,500 Wh	260 Ah	688	Five 140-watt modules
3,000 Wh	313 Ah	825	Six 140-watt modules

*12v battery equation: (Wh ÷ 12v) × 1.25 (80% discharge)
**Solar array watts equation: Wh × 1.25 (battery efficiency factor)h × 1.10 (module derate factor) ÷ 5 (sun hours)

All solar systems should use true deep-cycle batteries. These are designed for the slow, steady, and deep discharge suitable for powering household and workshop loads, such as lights, tools, and appliances. By contrast, car batteries and other SLI (starting, lighting, ignition) type batteries, deliver a huge blast of power to start the engine and then are immediately recharged by the running engine's alternator. Discharging a starting battery to 50% or even 80% of its supply, as you do with deep-cycle batteries, would quickly ruin such a battery.

Batteries commonly used in 12-volt solar systems include T-105 6-volt golf cart batteries, L-16 6-volt "floor sweeper" batteries, and 12-volt deep-cycle batteries (above).

There are three main types of deep-cycle batteries used in solar systems: lead-acid, nickel-iron, and lithium-ion.

Lead-acid batteries are the most commonly used type by far, due to their balance of performance, relatively long life, and reasonably low cost. *Flooded* lead-acid (FLA) batteries tend to be the cheapest, but they need to be topped up with distilled water on a regular basis, making them a maintenance issue. They also will leak if tipped over—a maintenance *and* safety issue. *Sealed* lead-acid batteries won't leak when tipped and are essentially maintenance-free. They come in two types: absorbed glass mat (AGM) and gel. Gel batteries are generally less durable and can be damaged (irreversibly) if not charged precisely as designed. That leaves AGM batteries as the general favorite in the solar world, even though they cost about twice as much as flooded types.

Nickel-iron (NiFe) batteries, also called Edison batteries, are made with a potassium electrolyte that is a less hazardous material than electrolytes in other battery types. Edison batteries are robust and durable and can last many times longer than lead-acid batteries, but they have a relatively low storage capacity for their size as well as a high rate of self-discharge and a low rate of efficiency. They're also more expensive and are much less widely available than standard batteries. Edison batteries are favored for their long life and relative immunity to overcharging and over-discharging, if for little else.

NOTE: Any battery requiring maintenance, including FLA and NiFe batteries, needs ventilation to expel explosive hydrogen gas produced by the electrolysis of water inside the battery. Enclosures for these batteries must include means for ventilation, and large banks may need an explosion-proof exhaust fan to adequately ventilate the gas generated.

Lithium-ion batteries for solar systems are in the same family as batteries used for cell phones, laptops, and electric vehicles. They offer many advantages over lead-acid batteries but are significantly more expensive, so the question to ask is whether the advantages are worth it for your specific application. Lithium batteries are about ⅓ the size and ½ the weight of lead-acid batteries with comparable storage capacity, making lithium particularly attractive for RVs and other portable applications where space and weight are important considerations. Lithium offers about twice the battery life of lead-acid, and lithium batteries can be discharged to 80% with no significant effect on longevity. That means fewer batteries to buy and less frequent replacement.

Lithium storage requires a sophisticated battery management system (BMS), which adds further to the overall cost. For large systems, lithium storage may be available as part of a manufactured system that couples batteries with the proper charging mechanism for ease-of-installation and to promote safety by ensuring only qualified individuals will work with these highly technical components.

Battery Ratings

When shopping for batteries, be aware that the amp-hour rating, or storage capacity, of a battery is based on the rate of discharge. A battery rated at 100 Ah when discharged over a 20-hour period may only deliver 80 Ah if discharged in a 10-hour period. Conversely, the same battery may deliver 130 Ah when discharged over 100 hours. Manufacturers provide specification sheets that list the expected capacity at a given rate, called the C Rate, and often include a dozen or more listed rates.

Another critical rating factor is cycle life, the number of cycles a battery can deliver. Discharging a battery (typically no more than 50 percent with lead-acid batteries) followed by a full recharge is one cycle. This rating varies by depth of discharge. For example, a battery may be rated for 1,500 cycles at 10 percent discharge per cycle but only 1,000 cycles at 50 percent depth of discharge, and still fewer at 80 percent.

One cycle per day is 365 cycles per year. When used daily, a 1,500-cycle battery should last about four years, under good conditions (see below). The labeled Ah amount for deep-cycle batteries typically is based on their 20-hour rate, but some batteries are advertised with their 100-hour rate, which can make them appear 30 percent larger when you compare only the labels, so be sure to look at the C Rate specifications. The 20-hour rate generally relates to a daily cycle rate.

Tips for a Long Life

Given the cost of quality deep-cycle batteries, it pays to take good care of them. Poor operating and maintenance habits can make a five-year battery last just one or two years. Here are some tips to stretch the life of your lead-acid batteries:

- Discharge batteries no more than 50% for maximum life; do not discharge more than 80%, which significantly shortens their life.
- Keep them cool: temperatures over 77°F dramatically shorten battery life.
- Maintain electrolyte levels in flooded lead-acid batteries, checking levels at least once a month. Overcharging/discharging batteries reduces electrolyte levels more quickly, requiring more frequent filling.
- Check battery cable connections regularly for looseness and corrosion; both lead to inefficiency and incomplete charging.

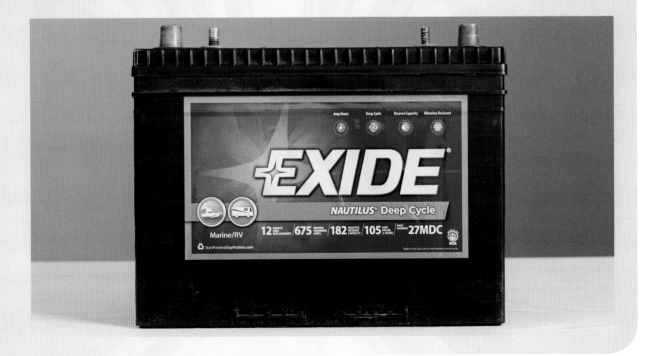

12-Volt Solar Light System

One of the easiest ways to put photovoltaic modules to work around your home is to purchase a self-contained kit. Kit contents and qualities vary, and if you apply the dollars-per-watt cost calculations most pro installers use, kits aren't the best value. But it's a very user-friendly way to jump into solar. If you have a garage or shed on the far reaches of your property and you'd like to convert it to useful work space where you can store and charge batteries, watch TV or play music, or just put in some overhead lighting for hobby work, a kit like the one shown here may be just the answer you're looking for.

The kit used in this project is a 45-watt, three-module PV kit purchased from a large discounter. In addition to the three 15-watt PV modules, it includes two 12-volt lights, battery hookups, a combination regulator/charge controller/safety fuse, and an adapter plug for different DC appliances. To complete the installation, the only missing elements are a roof boot to seal the roof penetration for the module wires (if you come through the roof) and electrical conduit for the wire leads from the modules. You'll need enough conduit to get from the back of the modules to just above the regulator/charge controller.

You can set this up as a battery charging station for car, boat, and RV batteries, or you can just install a permanent deep-cycle battery and use it to power a few lights and DC chargers and appliances. You can also use the system to power AC appliances and lights, but you'll need to add a power inverter with a minimum capacity of 300 watts.

The PV modules slip into angled mounting brackets that can be placed either on a flat surface or a pitched roof. If you are working on a pitched roof, follow all safety precautions for working at heights and wear fall-arresting gear if the pitch is steep.

With the PV modules and a charge controller in place, this solar power-generating station can do a lot more than just charge batteries, even without an AC inverter. Use it to supply power to a pond or waterfall pump, add a few DC lights, hook up garden lights, or just keep a few deep-cycle batteries charged up for emergency power in case the utility lines go down in a storm. If you live in the frozen north, it's also the perfect power source for an ice-fishing shack. Just plug in a DC-powered light, coffee maker, and TV and you're good to go.

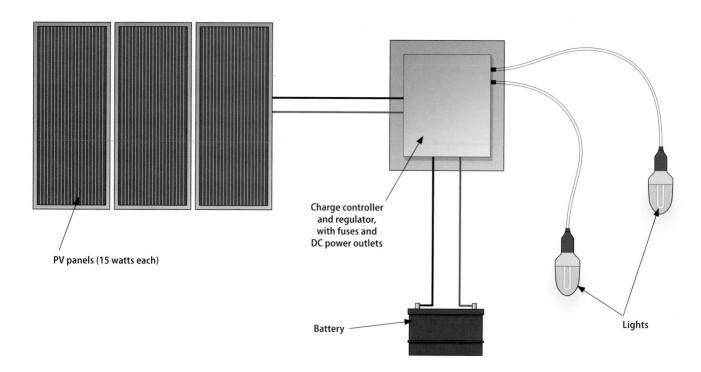

PV panels (15 watts each)

Charge controller
and regulator,
with fuses and
DC power outlets

Battery

Lights

Parts of this solar light kit include: three 15-watt photovoltaic panels (A); snap-in mounting stand (B); regulator (C); multi-purpose adapter (D); battery connectors (E); light wires (F); 12-volt LED lights (G). A 12-volt battery is required but not included with the kit.

☀ How to Install a 12-Volt Solar Light System

1 Locate the roof rafters, either by using a stud finder or by lifting up shingle tabs and tapping in finish nails. You must plan to fasten at least one of the angled mounting brackets to a rafter. If the other doesn't fall on a rafter, plan to attach it with toggle bolt anchors.

2 Predrill the holes for the mounting brackets (above), then fill them with roofing cement or silicone caulk (left). Fasten the brackets to the roof with neoprene screws (small lag screws with a rubber washer), or with toggle bolts if not attaching to a rafter.

3 Fit the bottom of the first collector module neatly into the slot in the mounting frame assembly.

continued on page 52

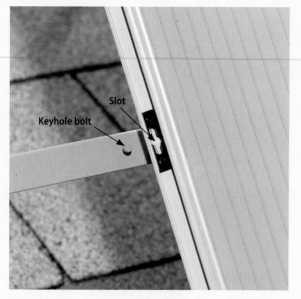

4 Lock the PV panel down into position by sliding the small bolt heads on the brackets into the keyhole slots on the back of the panel. (Other kits may use different fasteners.) Cover the panels with a drop cloth after they're in position–they'll start generating electricity as soon as the sun hits them.

5 Check the underside of the roof for electrical lines or ductwork. Locate an access hole for the panel cable into the roof deck, directly behind the panel assembly. Buy a flashing boot with a rubber boot sized for small electrical conduit (¾ or 1" is best—check online or at electrical or roofing supplier if you have difficulty finding one). Place the boot so that the top edge extends under two shingle tabs, then drill a test hole with a ¼" bit. Leave the bit in place and double-check the underside of the roof to make sure you come out in the right spot. If everything looks good, finish the hole with a hole saw or spade bit big enough for the conduit to fit through.

6 Cut a piece of conduit long enough to go through the roof and extend several inches above the boot. The conduit should continue on the underside of the roof over to the location of the regulator. Push the pipe through and hold it in place with a pipe strap or block of wood. Slip the roof boot over the pipe and wiggle it into place under the shingles. Spread roofing cement or silicone under the sides (but not the bottom) of the metal flashing, then nail it to the roof. Glue a 90° elbow to the conduit, turning it downhill, and extend with more conduit (if necessary) to the back of the PV assembly. Fish the leads from the panels through the conduit to the regulator; you may need to use an electrician's fish tape for this job. Finally, plug the opening in the conduit around the wires with electrician's putty or caulk to seal out bugs and drafts.

7 Install two sturdy shelves inside the building to hold the regulator and the battery. The shelf should be reachable by an adult so the equipment can be turned on and off and plugged into the adapter easily. The battery shelf should be at least 18" off the ground.

8 Connect the wires from the PV panels to the solar terminals on the back of the regulator/charge controller. Secure the wires to the walls or roof framing members to keep them clear. *CAUTION: The collector panels should be covered with a drop cloth or opaque material well before making these connections. Tape or clamp the drop cloth so it doesn't blow off.*

9 With the regulator turned off, fasten the battery leads to the back of the regulator, then clamp them to the battery posts— black to negative first, then red to positive. Then uncover the PV panels. Double-check the connections, then turn the regulator/ charge controller on. For a 12V battery, the voltage output reader will show 13 when the battery is fully charged.

10 This kit includes two DC lights. To install them (or other DC appliances), just plug the cord in to the proper port (or adapter) and turn the power on. Hang the 12-volt light fixtures from the rafters and then staple the cords to keep them secure and out of the way. Make sure to leave enough cord that the plug end is easy to insert and remove from the port. You'll plug and unplug the lights to turn them on and off.

Solar-Powered Security Light

The small system demonstrated in this project is relatively simple and is a great first step into the world of solar. The fact that the PV module, battery, and lights are part of a standalone system makes this a very easy project to complete. Many 12-volt DC systems do not require a system ground, but grounding is included in this overview to demonstrate the basic technique.

Your local building authority may or may not require a permit and inspections for a system of this type and size, so it's best to ask first. The project steps and system configuration shown here are for demonstration purposes only; always follow manufacturer specifications and local building code requirements for your own projects.

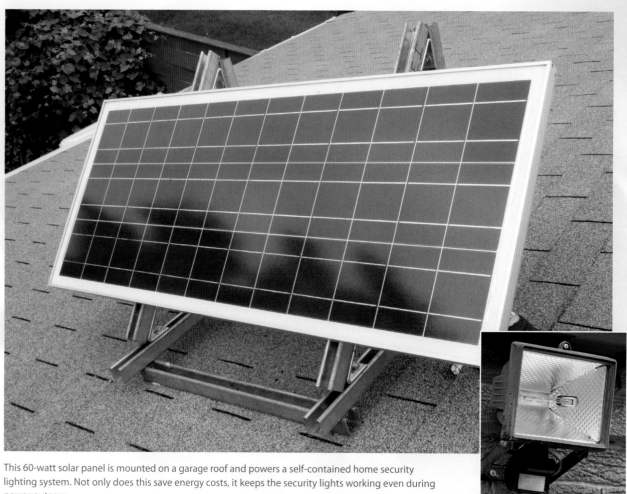

This 60-watt solar panel is mounted on a garage roof and powers a self-contained home security lighting system. Not only does this save energy costs, it keeps the security lights working even during power outages.

Schematic Diagram for an Off-the-Grid Solar Lighting System

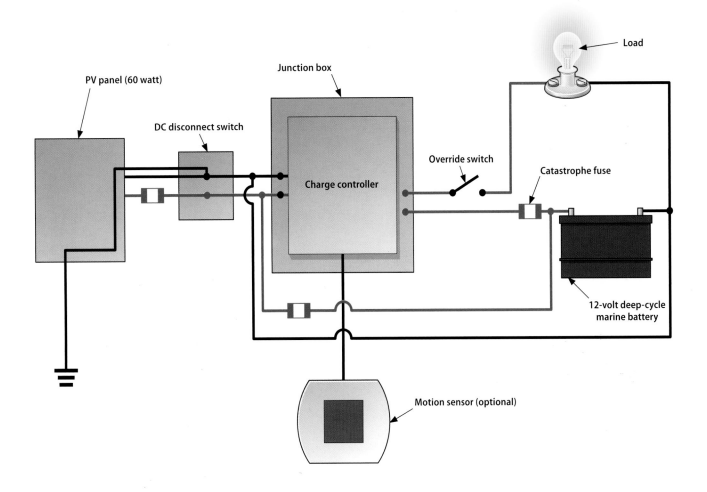

PV panel (60 watt)

DC disconnect switch

Junction box

Load

Charge controller

Override switch

Catastrophe fuse

12-volt deep-cycle marine battery

Motion sensor (optional)

TOOLS & MATERIALS

Tape measure
Drill/driver with bits
Caulk gun
Wiring tools
Metal-cutting saw
Socket wrench
Photovoltaic panel (50 to 80 watts)
Charge controller (12-volt, pwm;
    amp rating higher than solar module)
Catastrophe fuse
Battery sized for 3-day autonomy
Battery case
Battery cables
12-volt LED lights including
    motion-sensor light
Additional 12-volt light fixtures
    as desired

20' Unistrut 1⅞"-thick U-channel
    (see Resources, page 186)
45° Unistrut connectors
90° Unistrut angle brackets
Unistrut hold-down clamps
⅜" spring nuts
⅜"-dia. × 1"-long hex-head bolts
    with washers
Green ground screws
DC-rated disconnect or double throw
    snap switch
6" length of ½"-dia. liquid-tight flexible
    metallic conduit
½" liquid-tight connectors
Lay-in grounding lugs
Insulated terminal bars to accept one
    2-gauge wire and four 12-gauge wires

Cord cap connectors for ½"-dia. cable
½" ground rod and clamp
Copper wire (6- and 12-gauge)
Square boxes with covers
½" flexible metallic conduit
    or Greenfield
½" Greenfield connectors
11⁄16" junction boxes with covers
PVC 6 × 6" junction box with cover
14/2 UF wire
¼" × 20 nuts and bolts with lock washers
Roof flashing boot
Roof cement
Silicone caulk
Eye and ear protection
Work gloves

Mounting PV Modules

Cover the entire front of the module with a heavy drop cloth or bag secured with clamps. Leave the cover in place until the system installation is complete and ready to test. Position the solar module where it will receive the greatest amount of sunlight for the longest period of time each day—typically the south-facing side of a roof or wall. For a circuit with a battery reserve that powers two to four 12-volt lights, a collection module rated between 40 and 80 watts of output should suffice. These modules can range from $200 to $600 in price, depending on the output and the overall quality.

The stand components are held together with bolts and spring-loaded fasteners. The 45° and 90° connectors are manufactured specifically for use with this Unistrut system.

Connections for the feed wires that carry current from the collector are made inside an electrical box mounted on the back of the collector module.

An EPDM rubber boot seals off the opening where the PVC conduit carrying the feed wires penetrates the roof.

☼ Wiring a 12-Volt Lighting Circuit

1 Mount a junction box inside the building where the conduit enters from the module. Secure the conduit to the box with appropriate connectors. Run two 14-gauge wires through the conduit, leaving excess at the module and junction box. *OPTION: Using PVC conduit and electrical boxes instead of metal can reduce labor and materials costs and eliminate the need for grounding the metal conduit.*

2 Plan the system layout. Determine the placement of the battery and then decide where you will position the charge controller and DC disconnect. The battery should be placed at least 18" off the ground in a well-ventilated area where it won't be agitated by everyday activity. Mark locations directly on the wall.

3 Attach a junction box for enclosing the DC disconnect, which is a heavy-duty switch, to a wall stud near the battery and charge controller location. Use a metal single-gang box with mounting flanges.

4 Run flexible metal conduit from the entry point at the power source to the junction box for the DC disconnect box. Use hangers rated for flexible conduit.

continued on page 58

☼ Wiring a 12-Volt Lighting Circuit *continued from page 57*

5 Attach a double-gang metal junction box to the building's frame beneath the DC disconnect box to enclose the charge controller.

6 Attach the DC disconnect switch to the wire leads from the power source.

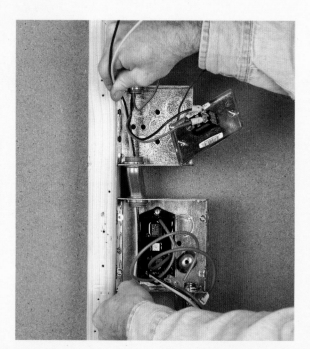

7 Install the charge controller inside the double-gang box. Run flexible conduit with connectors and conductors from the disconnect box and to the charge controller box.

8 Mount a PVC junction box for the battery controller about 2' above the battery location, and install two insulated terminal bars within the box.

9 Build a support shelf for the battery using 2 × 4s. The shelf should be at least 18" above ground. Set the battery on the shelf in a sturdy plastic case.

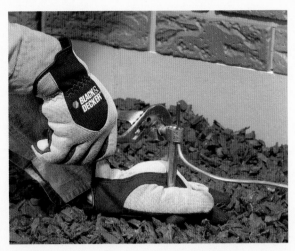

10 Set up grounding protection, if required. Pound an 8-ft.-long, ½"-dia. ground rod into the ground outside the building, about 1' from the wall on the opposite side of the charge controller. Leave about 2" of the rod sticking out of the ground. Attach a ground rod clamp to the top of the rod. Drill a ⁵⁄₁₆" hole through the garage wall (underneath a shake or siding piece) and run the #6-gauge THWN wire to the ground rod. This ground will facilitate lightning protection.

11 Wire the DC disconnect. Attach the two #14-gauge wires to the two terminals labeled "line" on the top of the DC disconnect switch.

12 Run wiring to the loads (exterior DC lighting fixtures in this case) from the charge controller. DC light fixtures (12-volt) with LED bulbs can be purchased at marine and RV stores if you can't find them in your home center or electrical supply store.

continued on page 60

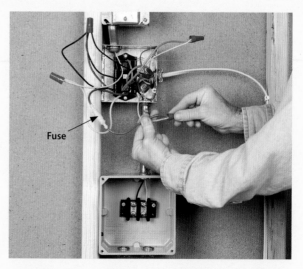

OPTION: Attach a motion sensor. Some charge controllers come equipped with a motion sensor to maximize the efficiency of your lighting system—these are especially effective when used with security lighting. The motion sensor is typically mounted to a bell box outside and wired directly to the charge controller with an 18-gauge × 3-conductor insulated cable. A system such as this can support up to three motion sensors. Follow the manufacturer's directions for installing and wiring the motion sensor.

13 Wire the charge controller. Route two more #14-gauge wires from the bottom of the DC disconnect terminals into the 4" × 1¹⁄₁₆" junction box and connect to the "Solar Panel In" terminals on the charge controller. The black wire should connect to the negative terminal in the PVC box and the red to the positive lead on the charge controller. Finish wiring of the charge controller according to the line diagram provided with the type of controller purchased. Generally the load wires connect to the orange lead and the red wire gets tied to the battery through a fuse.

14 Install the battery. Here, a deep-cycle 12-volt marine battery is used. First, cut and strip each of the two battery cables at one end and install into the battery control junction box through cord cap connectors. Terminate these wires on two separate, firmly mounted insulated terminal blocks.

15 Install the catastrophe fuse onto the positive terminal using nuts and bolts provided with the battery cables. Connect the battery cables to the battery while paying close attention to the polarity (red to positive and black to negative). Make sure all connections have been made and double checked.

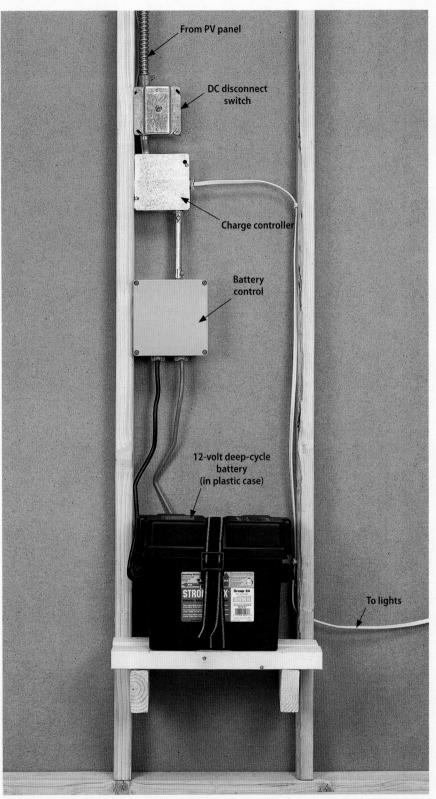

From PV panel

DC disconnect switch

Charge controller

Battery control

12-volt deep-cycle battery (in plastic case)

STRO X Group 24

To lights

16 Cover all junction boxes. Connect the 14-gauge wires at the solar module to the positive and negative terminals on the module. When you're ready to test the system, remove the cover from the module, and turn on the DC disconnect switch to complete the circuit. Test the lights and adjust the time to the desired setting.

Tip

If the battery control device does not include an easily accessible disconnect switch for the battery, add a switch to the positive battery cable (or positive battery terminal) between the battery and the control device or the charge controller. A disconnect switch allows you to cut power from the battery for servicing all other parts of the system. Without this shutoff, removing fused connections could create sparking.

Planning for Whole-House Power

Designing and installing a PV system that's large enough to provide most or all of household's electricity isn't a suitable DIY project for most people. There's a lot to learn about the equipment, the special connections and safety requirements, and how to optimize a system while staying within budget. Then there's the electrical work, the permit and inspections, and hooking up to the household system and the utility grid, which has to be done by a pro. That's why most homeowners opt for the turnkey service of a local solar installer and feel that the added cost is well worth it.

But even if you have no intention of getting up on your roof to mount your new solar panels, understanding the basics of home power systems can help answer a lot of key questions—things such as what type of system is best for you, how much power you need, and how much space that would occupy on your roof (or backyard). A simple assessment of your energy habits and your property will lead to a pretty good estimate of your basic system needs. Once you have that, you can get a ballpark figure of the cost of an installed system. And finally, there are plenty of resources for learning about rebates, credits, and other incentives available in your area.

One of the benefits of professional installation is that a good local installer will advise and guide you through all of these decisions when it's time to make them for real. He or she (or They) also will know about any incentive programs that will lower your total installation cost (it's good business for both of you). That said, if you're reading this book, you're probably the type who likes to do a little independent research before picking up the phone. This overview of system basics is a great place to start.

Designing a new house for solar power is ideal, as exemplified by this home's wide-open, sloped roof plane and large, south-facing windows. But an existing house doesn't have to be the perfect candidate to make large-scale solar power a good investment.

Types of Home Power Systems

There are three basic types or setups of PV home power systems: grid-tied, off-grid, and grid-tied with battery backup. Standard grid-tied is the simplest and by far the most common type of residential system, while off-grid typically is used when a home or cabin is far from utility service and/or total independence from the grid is a priority. Grid-tied systems with battery backup are the least common type but are gaining popularity with homeowners who can easily hook up to the grid but desire the independence and other advantages of being able to go off the grid temporarily.

Grid-Tied

In a grid-tied setup, the utility system serves as a backup to supply power when household demand exceeds the solar system's capacity or during the hours when the sun is down. This eliminates the need for batteries or a generator for backup and makes grid-connected systems less expensive and easier to maintain than off-grid systems.

Another advantage of grid connection is that when the solar system's output exceeds the house's demand, excess power is delivered back to the grid and the homeowner often gets credit for every watt produced, even if the energy is used in the home. This is called net-metering and is guaranteed by law in many states; however, not every state requires utility companies to offer it, and not all companies offer the same payback. Some simply let the meter roll backwards, essentially giving you full retail value for the power, while others buy back power at the utility's standard production price—much less than what they charge consumers.

The main drawbacks of being tied to the grid are that you still have to pay service charges for the utility connection even if your net consumption is zero, and you're still vulnerable to power outages. When the grid goes down, your system shuts down; you can't power your house directly from your solar array (although some inverters include a power outlet supplied by the array; see page 68). The most cost-effective way to provide emergency backup power with a grid-tied system is simply to use a generator, which would not be part of your solar configuration.

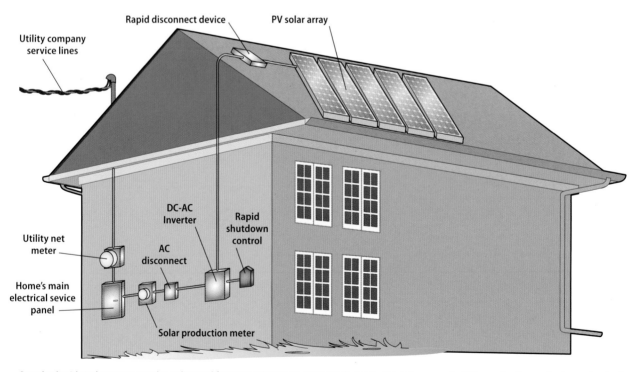

Standard grid-tied systems use the utility grid for "storing" excess power produced by the solar array. A utility production meter keeps track of all solar production and is used to calculate solar renewable energy credits (SRECs), where available.

Off-Grid

Off-grid systems serve as the sole supply of electricity for a home. They include a large enough array to meet the average daily demand of the household. During the day, excess power is stored in a bank of batteries for use when the sun is down or when extended cloud cover results in low output from the array. Most off-grid systems also have a gas-powered generator as a separate, emergency backup. In this case, the generator is wired to the solar system and can be used to charge the solar battery bank.

For anyone building a new home in an undeveloped area, installing a complete solar system to provide your own power can be less expensive than having the utility company run a line out to the house (beyond a quarter-mile or so, new lines can be very costly). There are some maintenance costs such as battery replacement, but it's possible to save a lot of money in the long run, and never having to pay a single electric bill is deeply satisfying to off-grid homeowners.

As mentioned, off-grid systems are a little more complicated than grid-tied setups. There are the batteries to care for, and power levels have to be monitored to prevent excessive discharge and to know when generator backup is required. To minimize power demands, off-grid homes tend to be highly energy-efficient. Installing super-efficient appliances is a major step toward making a smaller, less expensive solar array satisfy the home's energy needs.

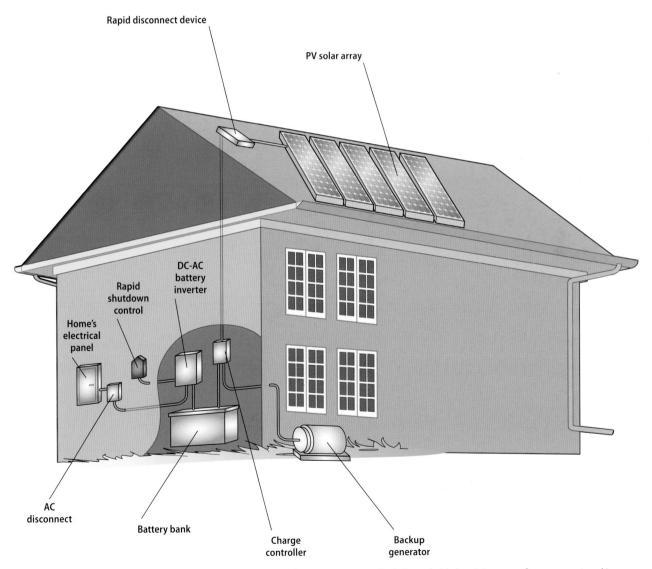

Off-grid systems are self-sufficient and have no connection to the power company. Daily household electricity comes from power stored in the battery bank, but a generator can provide backup power when the battery supply is low.

Grid-Tied with Battery Backup

Also called bi-modal or multi-modal, grid-tied systems with battery backup are a hybrid of grid-tied and off-grid systems. They connect to the grid and can supply power to the grid, and they can run independently from the grid, even during a power outage. They also can draw power from the batteries and the grid at the same time, allowing for "load shaving" to hedge against peak utility rates: During peak rate hours, the system can automatically draw some stored power from the battery bank so that less energy is pulled from the grid. The batteries get recharged later, during times of lower rates.

Bi-modal capability comes with extra equipment, based on the type of system. *DC-coupled* systems include a charge controller, which charges batteries directly from the solar array, and a battery inverter, which converts the DC power from the batteries to AC power for use in the house. These systems have the ability to power DC appliances without converting, in addition to standard AC loads. AC-coupled systems do not have a charge controller but have two inverters, one for the grid tie and one for charging the batteries. All bi-modal systems include a critical load panel that's used instead of the main grid-tied panel (the home's breaker box) to supply battery power during utility outages.

Freedom from power outages is the primary advantage to bi-modal systems, while the cost savings from load shaving vary by area and utility provider. On the downside, these systems are technologically complex, and the extra equipment adds significant potential replacement cost over the life of the system. The upfront cost for an installed system can be more than twice the cost of a standard grid-tied setup. DC-coupled systems are the original standard type, but some utilities do not allow them, as they can make it difficult to monitor solar production, a common requirement. Satisfying the rapid shutdown and arc-fault code rules (see page 79) can be problematic with DC-coupled systems.

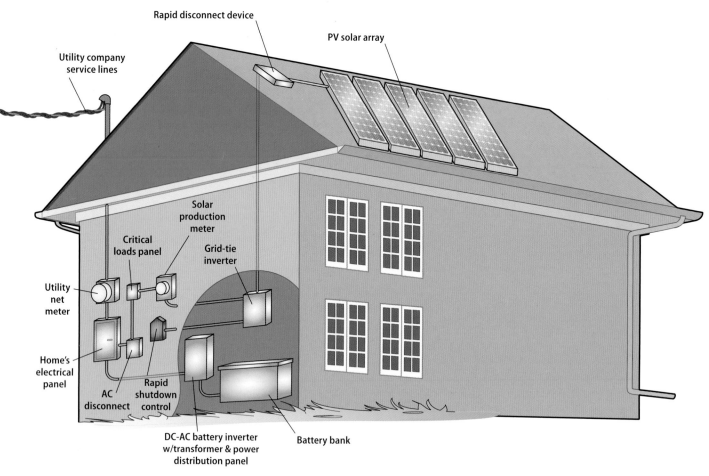

Grid-tied with battery backup systems have many of the same components of both grid-tied and off-grid systems and offer the essential capabilities of both systems. They are suitable only where utility service is readily available.

Home Power System Components

All of the working parts of a PV system—including the modules and mounting racks, inverters, safety switches, batteries, chargers, and wiring—are collectively known as the system equipment. This accounts for roughly half of the total cost of a professionally installed system, but it's essentially the core of your long-term investment, and getting a good return depends on the equipment lasting 25 years or more. That's no problem for quality modules or for basics such as racking and wiring. Inverters and other electronic components are likely to need replacement over the life of a system, and battery life is limited and highly variable, based on product quality as well as usage and maintenance habits.

Whatever type of system you're planning to install, it's important to choose quality components made by manufacturers that are likely to stay in business and can honor warranties for many years down the road. Compatibility is another consideration. Most modules will work with any system, but inverters, charge controllers, and other components may be compatible only with products from the same manufacturer. Solar equipment suppliers and solar installation pros can help you choose the right hardware for your needs and budget. The following is an overview of the major components you'll be shopping for, depending on your system type.

PV Modules

Solar modules were originally designed to charge 12-volt batteries, but today the great majority of standard full-size modules are used for grid-tied systems. A typical module for a grid-tie setup has 60 cells and a wattage output of 300 watts, although many other sizes and wattages are available.

Standard module width is 1 meter, or 6 cells wide, while module length varies by the total number of cells. Choosing a size is a matter of balancing output, efficiency, available space for the array, and cost. Modules with higher efficiency ratings and wattage output cost more but may allow you to use fewer modules overall. Note that improvements in efficiency have been slow to develop, and increases in wattage in recent years have more to do with increased module size.

Modules for off-grid systems are sized according to the system voltage. A 36-cell module (18 volts) is the optimal size for charging 12-volt batteries. Systems that run on 24 volts can use 36-cell modules wired in series, which doubles the voltage to 36 volts, or they can use 72-cell modules with an output of 36 volts.

Choosing mounting hardware for modules usually is a secondary decision, since most mounts work with many different modules. Mounting equipment and options are discussed on page 82.

Inverters

An inverter receives the DC solar power and converts it to AC power so it can be used by the household circuits and, with grid-tied systems, can feed the utility grid. Off-grid and bi-modal inverters are powered by batteries and do not connect to the solar array. Grid-tied inverters are powered by the solar array and cannot work with batteries.

Grid-tied systems may use one of three types of inverters. The historical standard is the central, or "string," inverter, a relatively large single unit that connects to the main power leads from the solar array. With this configuration, multiple modules are wired together so they output as a single unit. Each group of modules is called a string, and most systems have two or more strings feeding a single inverter. The inverter capacity must be equal to or greater than the total output wattage of the array. String inverters are the least expensive option, but the other two inverter types offer some key advantages.

Micro-Inverters

Micro-inverters are housed in small boxes that typically mount to the backsides of the solar modules or the racking below the modules. Each module gets one inverter, and the DC-to-AC conversion takes place at the module, so all of the power running between the array and the house hookup is AC power at standard household voltage. This is considered by some to be a safety improvement over string inverters, which receive DC power from the array at higher voltages.

Micro-inverters offer three key advantages over string inverters. First, they are able to monitor each module individually to maximize output for the entire array. This helps minimize efficiency losses due to shading or performance problems. String inverters see modules only as groups; if one panel is shaded or is malfunctioning, the inverter downgrades the entire string to match it, resulting in a greater loss of efficiency.

Another advantage is modularity. Since each module has its own micro-inverter, you can expand a system in the future without having to change other components. Micro-inverters also simplify installation on multiple roof areas. With a string inverter, expansion is limited by the maximum wattage rating of the inverter. If your array output is 3,000 watts and your inverter is rated for 3,500 watts,

Module sizes vary to fit spaces as well as power needs. These large 72-cell modules make the most of rooftop space that is too small for two 60-cell modules.

Micro-inverters are installed onto the module or the module mounting rack, then are connected to a cable (called a trunk cable) to form a branch circuit. A PV array may have one or more branch circuits, and each is joined to a junction box mounted to the module racking. *Enphase*

Solar optimizers, such as this unit from Solar Edge, offer a cost-savings benefit to solar arrays in areas of highly variable sun and shade. *Solar Edge*

you can add only 500 watts of output before you have to upgrade to a higher-wattage inverter.

Finally, micro-inverters do not require additional devices to meet rapid shutoff requirements (see page 79). When the grid power goes down, each micro-inverter automatically stops the outgoing current right at the module, so no connecting wires are energized.

The disadvantages of micro-inverters are cost, compatibility, and location. They cost more than string inverters, they're not always compatible with modules from different manufacturers, and their location on the modules means that if an inverter has a problem or fails, you may have to remove some neighboring modules to reach it (although this isn't usually a problem with ground-mounted arrays).

Power Optimizers

Power optimizers are connected to panels in order to turn them into smart panels so that they can produce more energy. In a solar energy system, each panel has its own distinctive point of maximum power output. Traditional solar energy systems prevent each panel from reaching its maximum production because differences between neighboring panels result in power loss. Power optimizers allow each panel to produce its highest potential energy. Power optimizers also offer improved safety with built-in module-level shutdown, eliminating the need for

additional devices to meet rapid shutdown standards. In addition, power optimizers enable full visibility into system production with module-level monitoring via a computer or smart phone. In combination with optimized inverters, power optimizers allow design flexibility so more modules can be installed, allowing for more savings on energy bills. Many optimizers even come with a warranty, such as this unit from SolarEdge (25 years!). Power optimizers keep the DC-AC inversion and grid functionality centralized at a central inverter, which helps to improve system profitability and reliability.

DC & AC Disconnects

Disconnecting devices are required for isolating individual pieces of equipment, including the solar array, both sides of the inverter, the charge controller and batteries, and the production meter. A disconnect is a rated switch, and often a fused junction box, with a manual switch or breaker that can cut the power between the current coming into and going out of the disconnect unit.

Most grid-tied systems include a DC disconnect (required as a rapid shutdown device within 10 feet of the array), which can isolate the PV array from the inverter, and an AC disconnect, which can cut power between the inverter and the grid connection and the house's service panel. DC disconnects may be located inside the house (not in bathrooms or closets), garage, or other structure. Utility- or code-required system AC disconnects must be mounted on an exterior wall in a visible and easily accessible location within 10 feet of the electric meter so that utility workers and emergency responders can quickly shut off the power to the grid and the household electrical system.

Disconnects typically are separate units, but some can be attached to string inverters, and some are integrated within inverter units. Disconnects are sized according to the output rating of the inverter (or inverters). They are critical components of any PV system but are simple electrical devices and are not a significant part of the hardware cost.

Production meters usually are installed near the inverter or the communication/connection hardware for micro-inverters. This can be indoors if allowed by the utility and local code authority. *Itron*

Solar Production Meter

A production meter is required by most utilities, solar financing entities, and local code authorities for all grid-tied systems. The meter measures the total output of AC power generated by the solar array before it goes to the service panel and into the home or to the grid. That data is used for billing, monitoring and customer presentment, remote service disconnect, and other operational efficiencies. If your system is eligible for energy credits, the production meter provides the energy data for calculating credits. Credit and certificate programs, as well as solar financing programs, typically require a "revenue grade" that meets specific performance standards. A production meter is used in addition to the utility-installed net meter that measures the net electricity usage of the house.

Local-access meters must be read on site and are the least expensive types. Remote-access meters can transmit data via the internet or cell phone networks so they can be monitored anywhere at any time. This capability may be required for code compliance or eligibility for energy programs.

Batteries & Charge Controls

Off-grid PV systems include large battery banks that may include a dozen or more batteries, plus a charge controller and monitoring devices to ensure optimal charging and discharging of the batteries. Grid-tied with battery backup systems also have battery banks as well as charge controllers or battery inverters for charging the batteries. See page 85 for more information on batteries and charge controllers.

For safety, a battery bank should be housed in a sturdy enclosure with a locking lid. Commercial enclosures are available, but most residential off-grid systems have simple wood enclosures. Some building authorities require that boxes are made with non-combustible lumber and sealed with fire caulk. Enclosures housing flooded lead-acid (FLA) and some other type of batteries must be ventilated and may require exhaust fans. Wood battery boxes for FLA batteries also may need a liner to catch any leaking electrolyte.

Sizing Your Home Power System

Determining system capacity is a question of demand and supply—figuring out how much power you use and how much you want to create with PV. You start by looking at a year's worth (or preferably two years' worth) of utility bills to find your annual electricity usage. Use this number and your home's geographic location for an initial size estimate, then use the PVWatts calculator on the National Renewable Energy Laboratory's website (pvwatts.nrel.gov) to refine your calculations.

Because system size translates directly to how much it costs and how much space the array occupies, it always makes sense to take a hard look at your electricity usage before settling on a system design. This is the time to identify and reduce waste. It might make sense to beef up a solar array to power an electric car, but adding capacity to meet the demands of inefficient lighting and appliances is like burning money for heat. See Lower Demand, Lower Supply (page 72) for some simple ways to reduce your energy loads.

Calculating a Grid-Tied Solar Array Size

Here's a sample sizing calculation for a standard grid-tied system that will generate enough power to offset the household's annual electricity usage. The initial steps assume the system will be installed on a house that's in full sun (no shading) with the array tilted due south at an angle equal to the latitude of the location (generally the ideal position). This provides an approximate array size to use with the PVWatts calculator.

NOTE: If you hire solar pros to install your system, they will likely use PVWatts or other modeling software and may also visit your site to assess your roof layout and consider shading and other factors that can affect system performance.

1. Add up your electrical usage for one year (or longer, if possible); your utility bill should report your monthly usage in kilowatt-hours (kWh):
   Example: 8,764 kWh
   Divide this number by 365 days:
   8,764 ÷ 365 = 24 kWh/day
2. Determine the sun hours of your location from the map (you can also search online for "annual average peak sun hours" for your city, or visit nrel.gov/gis/solar.html for additional map options). For this example, the house is located in Denver, CO, where the average peak sun hour figure is: 5.5 kWh/m2/day
3. Divide the daily electrical usage rate by the sun hours to find the *kW per sun hour* value:
   24 kWh ÷ 5.5 = 4.36 kW per sun hour
4. Factor in the *deration* (various efficiency losses known collectively as the "derate factor") from DC to AC grid power, conservatively estimated at 77 percent:
   4.36 ÷ 0.77 = 5.667 kW DC power array size

Therefore, the initial size estimate for the solar array is 5.667 kW or 5,667 watts of solar modules. However, this calculation assumes ideal south-facing conditions. Since most actual sites are less than ideal, the next step is to use PVWatts to fine-tune your estimate. You will need the slope of your roof and the azimuth direction your roof faces to complete the calculator; see tip (below).

Finding Slope & Azimuth

Slope is the angle of your roof. To determine slope, apply a strip of masking tape to a carpenter's level, 12" from one end. Set that end of the level onto your roof and hold the level perfectly horizontal. Use a tape measure or ruler to measure straight up between the roof and the tape on the level. This gives you the roof's rise over 12" of run. For example, a 5-in-12 roof slope rises 5" for every 12" of horizontal run.

Azimuth is the navigational direction of your rooftop. Find this using a standard compass or a compass app on a cell phone or other electronic device. Stand with your back to the roof plane that will receive the solar array, holding the compass or device directly in front of you. Read the compass to find the roof's direction. *NOTE: Adjust for magnetic declination, if using a standard compass; most compass apps automatically adjust for your location.*

5. Go online and open the PVWatts calculator (pvwatts. nrel.gov). Enter your home address, then confirm the selected location for weather data. Complete the System Info form as thoroughly as possible, using your estimated array size (5.667 kW in this example) for the DC System Size. The result gives you the annual output you can expect from the given system size at your location. You can experiment with various design parameters, such as array type and tilt, by going back and entering different inputs in the System Info form.

6. Determine the number of modules you need by dividing the array size by the module output rating; in this case, using the original system size and 280-watt (Pmp rating) modules:

5,667 watts ÷ 280 watts = 20.24 modules
This system would have 21 or 22 modules.

7. Estimate the inverter size using the total system output (for string inverter) or module output (for micro-inverters):
String inverter: rated at +/- 10% of array = 5,100 to 6,200 watts

Micro-inverters: 280 watts each; need one inverter for each module. *NOTE: Micro-inverters come in limited sizes, and you must confirm compatibility with the module manufacturer.*

Lower Demand, Lower Supply

The easiest way to lower the cost of a home power system is to reduce your daily consumption so you can meet your needs with a smaller system. You can find electricity waste in almost any household, and a little belt-tightening here can be a lot less painful than you might think. Assuming you're not heating the house or your hot water with electricity, the three big areas to look at are lighting, refrigeration, and air conditioning.

- Lighting is the simplest thing to improve. All of your lighting should be energy-efficient, preferably LED, which is six to ten times more efficient than conventional incandescent lighting and lasts many times longer. Compact fluorescents (CFLs) are fine if you already have them, but LEDs are more efficient, more reliable, and more durable, and in most cases produce better light quality. Don't confuse low-voltage with low-wattage; if it's not LED, low-voltage lighting is probably standard incandescent or halogen and is not energy efficient.

- Refrigeration: If you have an old fridge/freezer, compare its energy consumption to that of a similarly sized new model; the difference can be huge. Getting rid of an extra fridge or freezer in the garage or basement is an easy way to make a significant energy cutback.

- Air conditioning is the biggest electricity user in many households. If you live in a dry climate, an evaporative cooler is a viable alternative to conventional AC and uses considerably less electricity. Another alternative for relatively dry climates is a whole-house fan to quickly flush the house of hot air in the evening and morning. Ceiling fans help reduce the need for AC and are effective in all climates at any time of day.

- You can find out exactly how much power a fridge or any other plug-in appliance uses with an electricity monitor. Just plug the monitor into the wall outlet, then plug the appliance into the monitor to record every watt consumed by the appliance. Try this with your DVR/cable box; some of these use more power than a refrigerator!

Solar Economics

The potential return on your solar investment has a lot to do with where you live. Of course it helps to live in a sunny climate, but that's only part of the equation. Other location-specific factors that can impact the bottom line include:

- utility rates for grid-supplied power
- utility payments/credits for solar power
- government policies for solar installations
- state, municipal, and utility incentives
- local cost of solar installation and system hardware

These factors can be significant. Despite the enormous solar potential in the American southwest, solar electricity can be a better investment in parts of New England than in Phoenix, AZ.

Regardless of where you live, at some point you'll probably want to know how quickly your solar system

Sunny climates offer greater solar potential, reflected in the number of sun hours available each day, on average. The solar potential in most of Arizona is 7 to 7.5 sun hours per day, while the potential in Michigan is about half that, at 3.5 to 4.

will pay for itself. There are multiple ways to answer this question. One is the "simple payback" calculation: Divide the total cost of the system (after rebates/credits) by the monthly savings on your electrical bill (just the savings; not the total bill). For example, if the system costs $10,000 and it reduces your average bill by $100 per month, the system will pay for itself in 100 months, or less than 8½ years. Theoretically, any solar electricity you produce after that is free, barring maintenance costs.

Another method is to divide the installation cost by the total kilowatt-hour (kWh) production over the life of the system. This gives you the cost per kilowatt-hour for solar power, and you can compare that to what you're paying for utility power. For example, if your system is expected to produce 6,000kWh of power each year, multiply that by 25 years (the generally accepted lifespan for PV systems, although modules and other components likely will last much longer):

$$6,000 \times 25 = 150,000 \text{kWh}$$

If the system costs $10,000, your production cost is:

$$\$10,000 \div 150,000 \text{kWh} = \$0.0667 \text{ or about 6.7 cents per kWh}$$

Both of these simple calculations neglect maintenance and replacement costs over the life of the system. Inverters likely will need replacement in that time, and they can run upwards of $3,000 (for a string inverter; micro-inverters cost much less per unit but there are many more units that can fail). Maintenance costs should be minimal but can include the labor cost of removing and reinstalling a rooftop array if the roof ever needs major repair or replacement. Roofing aside, it makes sense to factor in the cost of replacing your inverter(s) at least once during the system's lifetime.

Rebates, Credits & Tax Breaks

The various financial incentives offered by federal, state, municipal, and utility-sponsored programs can take a big chunk out of your solar installation cost. Again, it depends on where you live and what's available when you install your system. You can learn about active programs from the Database of State Incentives for Renewables & Efficiency, online at dsireusa.org. Simply enter your zip code to see what's available in your area, and click on any single program to learn more details. Any experienced solar installation company will know about incentives available in your area.

In addition to notable state and local programs, here are two widely available programs you may have heard of:

Residential Renewable Energy Tax Credit: A federal program that offers a tax credit of up to 30 percent of eligible installation costs for PV systems, through 2019 (maximum benefit tapers to 26 percent for 2020 and 22 percent for 2021; expires at end of 2021). If your system costs $15,000 and is entirely eligible, you could get a $4,500 tax break on your federal income tax for the year the system is installed. If your taxes for that year are less than $4,500, you can carry over the remainder to the following tax year. *NOTE: Consult your tax advisor to confirm all tax benefits.*

Renewable Energy Credits (RECs): A renewable energy credit, or renewable energy certificate, is a credit you get for producing electricity with solar, wind, hydro, or other renewable source. RECs exist because once electricity is added to the national power grid—whether it was created by a coal plant, a wind farm, or a rooftop solar array—there's no way to tell where the power came from. The REC system allows the program authorities to track how much energy is produced by renewables and to reward those producers with the value of the RECs. Under the current program, producers receive one REC for every 1,000 kilowatt-hours (1 megawatt-hour) of electricity they produce.

You can think of it like a rewards program. If you create solar electricity, you can use that electricity in your home or you can sell it to your utility company. On top of that, you get a REC for every megawatt-hour you produce. So if your solar system produces 6,000 kWh per year, you get six RECs from the government, regardless of how much of that power you actually use in the house or sell to the utility.

RECs may be paid out monthly to homeowners in the form of $/kWh. For example, if the REC amount from the program is $0.04/kWh, the system owner receives 4 cents for every kWh the system produces over the contract terms (often 10 - 20 years), even if this energy is used in the home.

Net Metering: You may have heard net metering described as "running the meter backwards." It means you get charged only for the electricity you use, and you get credits for excess electricity that you supply to the grid, which is used by your neighbors. Depending on the program, you may get paid for these credits or they may simply be applied toward future electricity usage. These credits are not the same as RECs, which you get just for producing the electricity, no matter how much you use.

Net metering rules and rates are set by your state and/or utility company and vary widely. Some programs value outstanding electricity credits at the retail cost, while others buy excess power at the utility's production price, typically much lower than the consumer rate.

How to Find Out What Your System Will Cost

Once you have an idea of the size of system you need, you can talk with a few local solar installers to get a rough estimate, but don't expect actual quotes over the phone. To get an even quicker (and probably rougher) estimate, you can use an online calculator such as Solar-Estimate (solar-estimate.org). This calculator is provided by the Solar Energy Industries Association (SEIA; see page 186) and includes information on rebates and other incentives based on your location and utility provider. After filling out the calculator form, you can also opt to receive a call from a local solar installer in your area to discuss the quote you get from the calculator, to see whether it's realistic.

The cost for solar installations is often given as the price per watt of system output. For example, you might expect a starting price of $3 to $4 per watt, which means a 5kW system might cost around $15,000 to $20,000 before rebates and credits. If you live in an area with fairly favorable solar policies and programs, your final cost might be less than $10,000 for a 5kW professionally installed system.

Buy, Lease, or Finance?

If you're not ready or able to purchase a solar system out of pocket, you might consider financing or leasing options. When you finance through a solar company, you get a loan for the initial purchase of the system, and you pay it off over a specified period (say, 30 years) at a fixed interest rate (say, 4.5%). Assuming the system offsets all of the household electricity (averaged throughout the year), you can simply compare the fixed monthly payment on the loan to an average electric bill from the utility to see the difference.

Leasing a system is more like a rental agreement. The holding company installs the system on your property, often for free, and retains ownership of the system. With standard lease agreements, you make monthly lease payments and get the solar energy for free. With a power purchase agreement, or PPA, you pay for the solar electricity you use, at a specified rate. This rate typically is lower than the local utility's rate, but like the utility service it's also subject to regular increases, perhaps 2% or 3% per year. Some lease contracts include the option to buy the solar system during or after the lease period.

No matter how you pay for a grid-tied system, keep in mind that you'll always pay the going utility rate for any power that you pull from the grid. If your solar array offsets only 60% of your household power for the year, the other 40% will be priced at the current electricity rate—and that's on top of any monthly payment for financing or leasing the system. Also keep in mind that if you sell your house during the contract period, the agreement most likely will have to be transferred to the new owners.

Working with Solar Professionals

There are thousands of solar companies in the US, making for a highly competitive market for residential customers. This means you can expect great service and good prices no matter where you live, provided you find the right installer. There's no special trick to this, either—just the same due diligence you should perform before hiring any contractor for a major project. Look for reputable, experienced, licensed contractors who can refer you to plenty of happy customers. And, of course, get at least three bids or estimates for comparison.

Solar industry professional associations are excellent resources for information and help with finding local contractors. These include the Solar Energy Industries Association (SEIA; seia.org) and the American Solar Energy Society (ases.org) at the national level, as well as numerous state and local affiliates of these and other organizations. Many of these groups have directories that provide background and contact information for solar companies that belong to the association. Membership in a well-established, respected organization is no guarantee of quality service, but it's some indication of the companies' commitment to the solar business community, and many associations enforce a code of ethics for their members.

The reputation and reliability of your solar contractor are important considerations, but just as important is the stability of the original equipment manufacturers (OEMs) who produce the main components of your system and who carry those long warranties. Many of these are large, longstanding companies with expertise in energy and/or electronics, so it's a good bet they'll be around in 20 or 25 years to honor their product warranties. Always discuss warranties carefully with your solar contractor.

Services likely to be included in a contractor's system package are:

- Complete system design and installation
- Guarantees on workmanship/installation
- Obtaining permits
- Coordinating hookup with utility company
- Obtaining rebates and credits
- Help with OEM warranty claims
- Lifetime technical support

Be sure to ask about all of these items before signing a contract. For more information and tips for examining contracts and working with solar professionals, download a copy of SEIA's *Residential Consumer Guide to Solar Power* (see page 186), which includes specific questions to ask when considering lease agreements.

What Contractors Look For

In order to give you an accurate quote for your system hardware and installation, a solar contractor will look at three main factors:

1. **Location:** An installer will examine your house and property to help you determine the best option for locating your solar array, considering the area available, shading, roof slope, roofing material and its condition, and other factors. If your rooftop is not a good candidate, you can look at options for ground-mounting the array.

2. **Electrical demand:** You and the contractor will look over past utility bills to determine how much electricity you use and discuss how much you hope to produce with solar.

3. **Budget:** How much you want to spend on your system is directly tied to how much power you hope to produce. A bigger system will cost more up front but may allow you to offset most or all of your grid use over the year, while a smaller system will cost less initially but will add a higher percentage of grid power to your financial plan.

Permitting and Installation Process

Once you've hired a solar contractor, they will complete the system design and obtain all required permits and permissions for the project. A standard rooftop system will likely need building, electrical, and zoning permits, as well as an interconnection agreement from the utility company. Additional permissions may be required for homes with landmark status or to satisfy homeowners association rules or community covenants. States and municipalities with solar-friendly policies often have streamlined permitting processes, with programs such as one-page permit applications and same-day turnaround for standard installations. Permitting can be much more complicated—and expensive—in areas with less forward-thinking policies.

Your contractor also will apply for rebates and other financial benefits, as applicable. Tax credits are associated with your personal income taxes and are your responsibility. You should discuss all credits up front with your tax advisor so you fully understand the rules and your expected benefit.

Once the rooftop mounting brackets and rails are installed, placing the solar panels is a matter of patience and precision.

Installation Process

Here's the basic installation process for a standard grid-tied system with a rooftop array:

1. **Locating roof framing (rafters or trusses) and marking the layout for the mounting system brackets.**

2. **Installing mounting brackets and rails.** Each bracket typically is set on top of metal flashing and is anchored to the roof framing with a lag screw. The long metal rails that will hold the modules are bolted to the brackets to complete the racking system.

3. **Prepping for modules; varies by system.** If micro-inverters are used, they may be installed onto the mounting rails and connected to one another. Rails may be tied together with grounding wires. Installation of junction boxes for trunk cables may be installed onto the racking system or other rooftop location. Conduit and fittings are installed for running array cables through the roof or down the wall to the system connection point.

4. **Installing the modules.** Each module is tested for continuity to confirm there are no short circuits before or after it is set onto the racking and secured with bolted metal clips. Once mounted, modules are connected together, and to the micro-inverters, if used. All cabling is neatly tied up with zip-ties or other fastening system. The end of each module string (group of modules) is connected to a junction box, and cables are run from the array to the system connection point. There should be no visible sagging or loose wires when viewing under the array.

5. **Mounting component boxes.** Depending on the system, this may include a string inverter, electrical subpanel, production meter, AC disconnect, birdhouse (for rapid shutdown, see page 000), or combiner box.

6. **Completing the system wiring.** Running cables and connecting the array and all the system components typically is done by an electrician who works for or subcontracts with the solar installer. The solar system is connected to the household wiring system with one double-pole circuit breaker added to the home's main service panel (breaker box).

7. **Connecting to the grid and obtaining permission to operate (PTO).** After the system passes final inspection the installer applies for a new meter and permission to operate. Once approved, the utility installs a new meter and delivers a PTO letter. Only then are you allowed to bring your system online and begin producing and using solar electricity.

Installation can begin only after the permits are obtained and posted at the work site. A typical rooftop installation may take only three to four days, depending on factors such as system size and complexity, rooftop and solar array configuration, roofing material, and the mounting system. Large ground-mounted systems often require extra time for building the mounting structure and running the cabling underground to the house.

Despite the typically quick installation, the time between hiring an installer and using your new system to produce electricity can easily be three months or more. Most of this delay lies in processing the paperwork through the utility and building authorities and varies by location. Discuss the timeframe with your installer up front so you know what to expect.

Common Code Rules

Ensuring your system is code-compliant is the job of your solar installer (and the building inspector), but it might help to be familiar with a few of the major code issues that can restrict and/or add complexity and cost to your system's design and installation. Most solar code rules are based on section 690 of the National Electrical Code (NEC), which includes minimum requirements for residential solar systems.

Mobile Solar: RVs, Boats & Portable Power

The inherent advantages of solar electricity make it particularly ideal for portable applications…

- Silent operation
- Zero emissions
- Works anywhere there's sunlight (no need for shore power)
- No moving parts; minimal risk of breakdown
- No fuel to carry and store

…and you can store power in batteries for when the sun goes down.

RVs may benefit the most from solar because they can support sizable systems that provide power for the essential comforts and conveniences of a home on the road. The silence and portability of solar make it a natural fit for life on the water, too, where the sun is plentiful, and problems with shading and module positioning can be easy to solve. Portable solar systems, including small, pullable carts and larger, trailer-mounted setups, let you bring power to a work site, campground, picnic area, or just deep into your own backyard. Small systems also can be great DIY projects that teach you the basics of battery-based solar power.

Mobile PV systems typically are 12-volt and have the same main components as a simple DC system for an outbuilding. One or more modules are used to charge batteries via a charge controller, and the batteries supply power directly to DC devices or to AC devices via an inverter. System capacity is determined by the output of the modules and the storage capacity of the batteries. The only safety devices needed are fuses and perhaps a breaker or other type of switch for cutting power from the modules.

This section covers the basics of 12-volt systems for RVs and boats, and shows some possibilities of what you can do with portable systems that can be rolled anywhere you need power. There's also a DIY project for turning a heavy-duty garden wagon into a portable power center. Installing a larger system on an RV or boat may or may not be a feasible project for a DIYer; this is something to discuss with the vehicle manufacturer and your solar equipment supplier.

Solar power allows you to boondock in peace, without the noise, fumes, or refueling of a gas-powered generator.

RV Solar

RVs represent a small portion of the general solar market, but they're the heart of the market for 12-volt solar equipment. This means you have a lot of choices for products and system configurations. In some cases, what works well on a house or outbuilding works equally well on an RV. In other cases, the unique installation and operating environment—not to mention the realities of the road—dictate the best products to consider.

Solar Modules & Mounts

The durability and relatively high efficiency of standard rigid modules make them the all-around best choice for RV installations. Durability is important for standing up to storms of all kinds as well as tree branches and other hazards of nature. Efficiency is particularly important for RV applications because of limited space: higher-efficiency modules produce more power at smaller sizes.

Framed rigid modules can be mounted to roofs with metal brackets that hold the panels a few inches above the roof surface. This creates an air gap that helps reduce the very high temperatures on vehicle roofs, which lower a module's efficiency. Adjustable mounts allow for level installation on sloped or rounded roofs. Mounts with

Lower-profile rigid mounts are designed for secure permanent mounting of modules. Some, such as the one above, are intended to be attached only when the vehicle is parked, and they can be combined with other power sources (even alternative sources such as wind).

tilting capability let you tilt up the modules to maximize solar potential.

Flexible modules have left the market for residential systems, but they've found a home in the mobile world, for a couple of reasons. They are thin (about ⅛ inch thick) and lightweight (just a few pounds for a full-size module) and can be flexed up to 30 degrees to conform to curved rooftops. Installation options include glue-down, screw-down, and grommet systems that simplify removal. They are durable enough to be walked on, hailed on, snowed on, etc., but they aren't as durable as the tempered glass surfaces of rigid panels.

There are other drawbacks, too. Flexible modules traditionally offer only 6 percent to 8 percent efficiency, compared to 14 percent to 18 percent with rigid modules, although these numbers apply to amorphous construction; some newer flexible units are made with crystalline silicon and offer somewhat higher efficiency. Also, flexible modules can't be tilted, limiting their overall output potential.

Charge Controllers & Inverters

All battery-based solar systems need a charge controller to regulate the flow of electricity going to the batteries. Charge controllers help to prolong battery life, prevent overcharging, and maximize system performance, among other things. A good controller can make a big difference in your day-to-day electricity budgeting.

Shunt-type, or "On-Off," charge controllers have been the traditional standard for 12-volt RV systems, but newer series-type controllers with pulse width modulation (PWM) offer some advantages, including keeping the batteries topped off at a higher charge and reducing problems with water loss and sulfating that are common with shunt-type controllers. Series controllers with maximum power point tracking (MPPT) are capable of charging "boosts," which use excess voltage from the modules to increase the charging amperage, maximizing the charge particularly early and late in the day, when the modules are relatively cool and the battery voltage is low.

If you want to charge your cell phone or laptop or run any appliance that plugs into a standard 110/120-volt wall outlet, you'll need an inverter installed on your system. Inverters used in RVs are the same types used on many other 12-volt systems. The best types are pure sine units, which will power any AC device just as well as standard household power. Modified sine inverters can cost about half as much as pure sine, but many appliances, such as refrigerators, microwaves, and electrics, don't run as smoothly or efficiently on modified sine power. Choose an inverter size based on the total power demand of all the appliances you'd like to run at the same time. If you exceed the wattage rating or the amperage of the inverter's breaker, the power will shut off.

Rigid solar modules are durable and efficient, which makes them a good choice for RVs with a flat roof. Fliexible modules that are very thin (⅛") and flex to follow a profile up to 30° make sense atop some RVs that have round roofs.

Battery Remotes & Monitors

A battery remote meter works in conjunction with the charge controller and includes a display and indicator lights that show you the charging amperage, battery voltage, and charging status of your batteries in a convenient location. A battery monitor provides much more detail about battery status and condition, including percent-full, specific voltage for multiple batteries, and real-time amperage, which shows the wattage or amperage as it is coming into and going out of the batteries. This allows you to see how much power each light or appliance is using: turn a device on or off and note the rise or fall of the discharge rate. Monitors also record data so you can review the history of recent charge/discharge cycles and keep track of lifetime amp-hour discharge.

Battery monitors are optional devices but are considered essential for long-term off-grid living on solar power. By giving you detailed information about charge/discharge status, monitors tell you how much reserve power you have at all times, and they help you avoid excessive discharge, which dramatically shortens the life of your expensive batteries. You can buy a battery remote and battery monitor separately, or you can choose a combined unit that includes the functions of both.

Batteries

Most RV solar systems still use lead-acid AGM batteries, but lithium-ion is slowly moving into the market. Lead-acid batteries must be true deep-cycle type, not marine batteries that are designed for starting engines as well as running lights and appliances. A starting or cranking battery is not needed because, unlike boats, RVs typically have separate batteries for the vehicle engine and the "house" power provided by the solar system.

Lithium batteries offer some key advantages over lead-acid, including longer life, deeper discharge, faster charging, and more capacity in a smaller size. Lithium batteries don't need to be stored in a ventilated compartment, but they should stay within their optimal temperature range to ensure maximum battery life. This is an important consideration if your vehicle will be subject to wide temperature swings and extreme climate changes. The most obvious downside of lithium is the cost, at about two to three times higher than lead-acid batteries. See page 46 for a discussion of battery types and performance for solar systems.

Sizing an RV Solar System

Sizing a solar array for an RV is similar to sizing for household power: look at your normal consumption habits and determine how much solar you need to provide that amount of power. With a house, you can simply refer to your electricity bill; with an RV, you have to look at how quickly your batteries run down on a typical day. You can do this by simply starting with fully charged batteries, then using electricity normally until the batteries are discharged—down to about 50 percent for lead-acid batteries or 80 percent for lithium-ion.

For example, if your battery bank can deliver 200 amp-hours before hitting 50 percent full, and it takes two days of normal usage to hit that mark, you typically need 100 amp-hours per day of power. Use that number as the minimum production goal for your solar system.

This simple method is suitable for rough estimation, but for much greater accuracy you can install a battery monitor before conducting your consumption test. The monitor will tell you exactly how much power is drawn from the batteries so your results won't be based on the estimated capacity of your battery bank. You can also learn how much power is consumed by various appliances, which can be helpful to know in any case but also can help you decide whether to keep those appliances or to replace them with more efficient models or substitutes—before you settle on a system size. Be sure to use a quality battery monitor that includes a shunt in its wiring. Others only measure voltage with percent-charge reading, making it difficult to calculate energy use.

Marine Solar

Solar systems for marine applications range from very simple, portable kits that keep batteries topped up during mooring to more powerful setups with rigid modules that can fully recharge batteries and provide additional power for running lights and appliances on board. Larger systems typically are used to reduce the need to recharge by engine power, but it's possible for boats without engines to rely solely on solar for electricity. Standard marine solar is 12-volt, and most systems are simple enough for DIY installation.

Solar Modules

Modules for boats come in a variety of types and sizes to suit many different installation options. Small units are designed for portability and easy storage and include both rigid and foldable or rollable versions. You simply take them out when they're needed and set them in a sunny spot. Modules that output less than 1 amp typically don't need a charge controller and can be plugged directly into a 12-volt outlet or hooked up to battery terminals for trickle-charging. The circuit should have a fuse located near the battery.

Choose a module size for trickle-charging based on your battery capacity:

module output (in milliamps; mA) ÷ 2 = battery capacity (in amp-hours)

For example, a 200mA module is suitable for trickle-charging a 100-amp-hour battery (which requires about a 3.6-watt module).

Larger modules for boats may be rigid framed panels or flexible modules, typically with 30 or 36 cells. Rigid modules usually are permanently mounted to metal racking or clamped to rails or posts with special fittings. They can also be suspended with cables, allowing the module to be tilted toward the sun at any angle. Flexible modules can be tied down almost anywhere, making it

Small modules for trickle-charging are designed to go almost anywhere and often come with cables, fuses, and terminals for easy hookup to batteries or a 12-volt outlet.

easy to move or stow them as needed. The flipside of this versatility is that flexible modules offer lower efficiency, so you need larger or more modules to get the same output as rigid units.

Depending on the module output and the configuration of larger systems, modules may be hooked up to a 12-volt circuit, with fuses near the battery and the module, or they may connect to a circuit breaker in the vessel's DC distribution panel.

Charge Controllers & Batteries

A charge controller is recommended for solar modules with an output of 1 amp (12 watts) or more. Charge controllers are rated in amps to match the total module output. Small controllers may be called "regulators" and often are designed for charging a single battery or small bank. Larger units usually can charge one or two battery banks and may include features such as maximum power point tracking (MPPT) to maximize the charging current and boost the charge during relatively low production times.

Rigid modules can be mounted on the pushpits at the side or end of a boat or overhead on a pole system. A simple pivot mechanism helps maximize production and allows the modules to swing down close to the boat when they're not needed.

Flexible modules are thin and lightweight, in addition to being flexible, so they can go where rigid panels can't. Most flexible units have a grommet at each corner for easy tie-down.

As with all battery-based solar systems, true deep-cycle batteries offer the most storage capacity and longest life and are therefore the best type for solar systems. Many boats have two battery systems, one that uses a starting battery for starting the boat's engine and another that uses a deep-cycle battery for supplying the "house" electricity. If a boat has only one battery system with one type of battery, it's usually a dual-purpose battery that offers the high starting amperage of a starting battery and can withstand deep discharges like a deep-cycle battery. However, dual-purpose batteries offer less capacity than deep-cycle batteries, so they're recommended only for small boats with limited house power loads and for boats that use two dual-purpose batteries for both starting and house power.

Get Out of the Shade

There's a lot of solar potential out on the open water. No trees to worry about, and boats or modules often can be moved to face the sun for maximum production. But it can be tough to find a spot on a boat that isn't at least somewhat shaded by a canopy, sail, mast, rigging, or other piece of essential equipment. Even a little bit of shading can make a big difference in electricity production, especially with the small modules (and smaller energy margins) of most marine systems. Here are some tips for maximizing production when it counts.

Stay out of the shade: Move portable modules as often as needed to keep them in full sun throughout daylight hours, particularly during the two or three hours before and after noon. Choose mounting locations for fixed modules carefully to avoid shading.

Use adjustable mounts: Rigid modules of all sizes can benefit from adjustable mounts that let you rotate and tilt the modules to face the sun.

Flatten flexibles: A module wrapped around your sail may be conveniently out of the way, but it won't capture as much solar energy as when it's laid flat.

Keep modules cool: All solar modules lose efficiency when they heat up (rigid lose more than flexible). Provide ventilation space behind modules to allow for airflow that helps keep temperatures down and minimize this efficiency loss.

Adjustable mounts are available for sizable rigid modules as well as small portable panels. Mounts that rotate and tilt (or use ball joints for infinite adjustment) are the best for maximizing capture throughout the day.

Portable Power

RVs and boats demonstrate that solar electricity can be completely portable and work without the utility grid or a shore hookup. But you certainly don't need a large vessel such as a boat or a land yacht to support a PV system. Any vehicle that can carry a solar module, a battery, and a charge controller can become a mini mobile power plant.

A garden cart makes a handy charging station or portable power center for picnics or backyard work or parties (see page 90), while a towable trailer can supply power for job sites and large outdoor events. If you don't have to lug around a battery, you can skip the cart or trailer and simply bring the solar to the battery with a portable charging kit.

Solar trailers are commonly used for construction, disaster relief, outdoor events, and all kinds of work in remote locations. Enclosed trailers may include extra space for tool and equipment storage as well as a small office space.

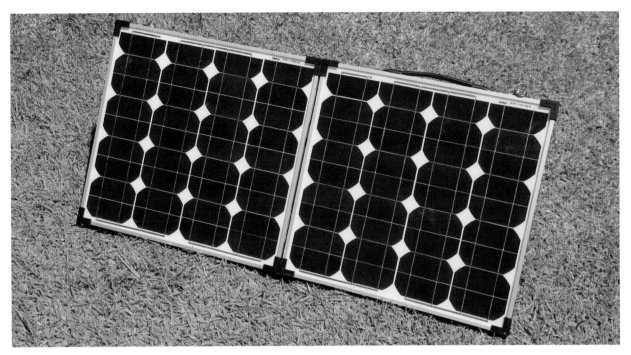

Portable solar charging kits include a foldable solar module with built-in charge controller and cables for battery hookup. Adjustable legs let you tilt the module toward the sun for optimal production. *Getty*

Personal solar chargers come in clever packages, such as this backpack-mounted trickle charger. *Getty*

Solar Power Cart

This solar power cart is a fully functional, completely off-grid, 12-volt solar system on wheels. Just roll it out into the sun to charge the on-board battery, and it's ready to go anywhere you need power. An AC inverter includes outlets for plugging in tools and power cords, while a DC power strip has ports as well as a USB connection for recharging phones, laptops and other electronics. The options are easily expandable to include DC ports or additional AC outlets. The module used for this system is a 100-watt, 12 volt solar crystalline panel with output amperage of up to 8.5 amps.

The cart itself is a heavy-duty metal utility cart with inflatable tires, the type commonly sold at home and garden centers. A cart with a flat bed and removable sides is ideal for solar conversion. The metal-mesh bed makes it easy to bolt down the structural parts and system components, and removing the sides allows you to build beyond the bed area while maintaining a low profile for stability. You can substitute with another type of cart as long as it's laterally stable and can easily carry 200 pounds.

Nearly everything about this project is customizable, including the system capacity and specific components, the system layout, and the module angle, which you'll want to optimize for your geographic location. You can also modify the basic wood structure shown here, by adding hinged plywood doors to enclose the battery area, or even a small roof behind the panel to provide some weather protection.

An inexpensive garden utility cart can be outfitted with a rigid solar module and a little equipment to deliver AC or DC power anywhere in walking distance.

CUTTING LIST

KEY	NUMBER	DIMENSION	PART	MATERIAL
A	6	1½ × 3½" × cut to fit	Support leg	2 × 4 lumber
B	1	¾" × cut to fit	Back panel	¾" plywood
C	1	¾" × cut to fit	Bottom panel	¾" plywood

Solar Power Cart Components

The cart's electrical system, as shown, includes the following main components. A few optional components you may want to add are discussed below as well.

1. **Solar module:** Standard rigid module designed for rooftop or ground mounting. Choose a module based on voltage output and overall size. A typical 100-watt module measures around 26 × 48 inches—a good size for a standard utility cart. A larger module, such as a 140-watt, will charge the battery faster but may be about 10 to 12 inches longer.

2. **Charge controller:** A basic PWM-type charge controller (shown here) is sufficient, but if you are able to spend the money a unit with low voltage disconnect (LVD) capability is a wise upgrade. An LVD controller automatically shuts off the outgoing power if the battery reserve gets too low, preventing battery damage due to excessive discharge. Most AC inverters will shut off at low voltages, but any DC outlets and other devices in the system will continue to discharge without LVD protection. Size according to chart below. *NOTE: The DC loads must be powered through the charge controller for the LVD to work.*

3. **Battery:** Deep-cycle battery or batteries suitable for a 12-volt system. See pages 000-000 for more information on battery types and capacity. AGM or gel-type batteries are recommended due to their low maintenance. One or two 12-volt batteries (wired in parallel) or two 6-volt batteries (wired in series) will work.

4. **Breaker/battery switch or inline fuse:** If running multiple circuits, select a circuit breaker with manual switch for disconnecting everything downstream of the battery. Size according to the chart below. For a single line you can protect the other components with an inline blade fuse (inset photo), but these devices cannot be used as a shutoff switch.

5. **OPTIONAL:** If you are planning to run multiple circuits, include a simple automotive fuse box or a marine-type, waterproof fuse box (shown) with blade-type fuses to protect all of the loads. Choose an appropriate fuse for each circuit load; some examples are shown in the wiring diagram on page 000.

6. **OPTIONAL:** Inverter: Required for powering AC tools and other devices. For heavier duty applications with multiple plug-ins, choose a pure sine wave inverter. For lighter duty you can use a cigarette-lighter plug DC/AC inverter (shown). Size according to chart below.

7. **OPTIONAL:** DC outlets: Multiple outlets or a multi-outlet strip with USB ports and standard 12-volt power socket(s). Each outlet is connected on its own fused circuit.

8. **OPTIONAL:** Negative bus bar: Standard marine bus bar for consolidating negative circuit wires and bonding to metal cart frame. Should include at least eight terminals and have an amperage rating equal to or greater than the charge controller's rating.

CHART: AMPERAGE RATINGS

Choose amperage ratings for your charge controller, inverter fuse (in system fuse box), and battery circuit breaker/switch based on the inverter's wattage rating.

200-watt inverter: 20 amps
300-watt inverter: 30 amps
400-watt inverter: 35 or 40 amps
500-watt inverter: 50 amps

The circuit for a simple solar charging station is fairly basic. The electrical charge comes form the module, through an inline fuse and enters the charge controller. The charge controller is connected to the terminals of a deep-cycle, 12-volt battery. A power lead from a cigarette-lighter style DC plug goes to the output terminal on the battery. An AC inverter containing an AC plug and a USB port is plugged into the DC plug.

TOOLS AND MATERIALS

Tape measure
Ruler
Circular saw
Drill driver
¼" drill bit
Utility cart (min. 200-pound capacity)

2 × 4 lumber
¾" exterior plywood, 3 × 3 feet
¾", 1½", 2", and 3" wood screws
3½" carriage bolts with nuts
　and large washers
Solar module

Module mounting brackets (4)
Charge controller
AC inverter
Inline fuse
Deep-cycle battery with cables
Battery tray with tie-down

1 Design the support legs to fit the cart and your solar module. Remove the sides from the cart and measure the usable width and length of the cart bed. The bottom of the triangular support legs should equal the width of the bed. Determine the latitude of your location by searching online with the name of the nearest large city. The latitude is the tilt angle at which to set the top (the hypotenuse) of the support triangle. The vertical side of the triangle should extend straight up from the bottom to the hypotenuse and will be beveled at the tilt angle. The bottom of the hypotenuse will be beveled at the tilt angle minus 90° (for example, if the title angle is 40°, the bevel angle is 50°). Draw the support on paper, using a protractor to establish the angle and scaling the drawing at ¼ size (1" actual = ¼" in drawing). Measure the length of the hypotenuse to make sure it will be long enough to fit the solar module and its mounting brackets. If necessary, extend the hypotenuse beyond the vertical side.

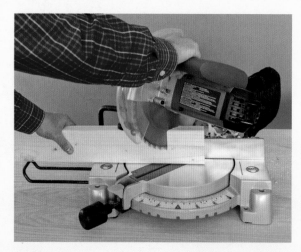

2 Construct the support legs with 2 × 4 lumber. Bevel the top end of the vertical side, using a circular saw set at the tilt angle. Cut the bottom end of the hypotenuse at the tilt angle minus 90°. *TIP: If your saw base won't tilt far enough, mark the side edges of the board at the desired angle. Set the saw blade for a straight (90°) cut and at full depth. Cut along the line on one edge of the board, then flip the board over and cut along the opposite edge.* Drill pilot holes, and assemble the two leg triangles with 3" screws.

3 Cut ¾" plywood for the back and bottom panels of the support structure. Fasten the plywood to the backs of the vertical leg pieces and the tops of the horizontal pieces, using 2" screws, to complete the structure assembly. Set the structure onto the cart bed and mark the locations for four or more mounting bolts. Remove the structure and drill ¼" holes for bolts through the plywood base and bottom support legs. Mount the structure to the cart with 3½" carriage bolts and nuts, using large washers to span the holes in the cart mesh.

4 Install the module mounting brackets onto the support legs, using 1½" screws, then test-fit the module. *NOTE: Leave the module covered with a tarp for safety; it will produce power even when exposed to artificial light. Determine the positions of the system components, including the battery, and mark the locations of holes for wiring runs through the plywood back panel. Also drill a hole through the base panel for a bonding wire between the bus bar and the cart bed.*

WARNING: Use only insulated tools when working with batteries. Touching both battery terminals with an uninsulated metal tool is extremely dangerous.

5 Install the battery tray and bus bar onto the plywood bottom panel over the cart bed. You may want to remove the solar module for easier access to the bed area. *TIP: Paint the plywood with exterior-paint to protect the wood.*

6 Connect the system components following the manufacturers' instructions and using the specified type and gauge of wire for each. Connect everything except the battery and the solar module. Set the battery into its tray and secure it with the included strap or clamping system. Connect the battery to the charge controller. Complete the final connections by reinstalling the solar module (if you removed it) and connecting the module leads to the charge controller, as directed by the manufacturer. Confirm that all wiring connections are made securely and correctly, checking for proper polarity on each component. Remove the cover on the solar module to test the system.

SOLAR HEAT

Unlike photovoltaic panels, solar collectors are everywhere around us. In fact, we're living on one. The Earth itself is one giant collector, absorbing light from the sun and keeping just enough of it under an insulating layer of atmosphere for life to exist.

Solar collectors work in a similar way, and although the scientific explanation for what they do is complicated, actually making one is not that difficult. There are basically two ways to collect solar heat and put it to a useful purpose, and we'll show projects that illustrate each type. The first is probably the simplest and most familiar, especially if you've ever owned a car with a black interior and left it parked in the sun with the windows rolled up. Dark colors absorb heat, and if they're in a space covered with glass much of the heat will be trapped, then come blasting out when you open the door. That's the principle behind the solar hot air collector on page 141. Solar hot water collectors take the idea a step further, by transferring that stored heat to water flowing through heat-absorbing pipes (see page 115), after which it can be used for hot water or heat throughout the house, or even stored for later use (page 130).

The second method is a little different. Instead of just absorbing heat in a black box, solar energy is first concentrated and focused by a reflective surface. This can be a curved, highly polished array of mirrors capable of generating heat measuring in the thousands of degrees, or it can be reflective foil glued to the slanting sides of a box, bouncing enough solar heat towards a black pot to cook a chicken dinner (page 97).

Either way, solar heat collectors have one big advantage over PV panels— a faster return on your investment, especially if you make your own.

IN THIS CHAPTER:

- Solar Ovens
- Solar Water Heater
- Solar Hot Air Collector—Window Mount
- Solar Hot Air Collector—Roof Mount
- Solar Still
- Solar Lumber Kiln

A large array of solar hot water collectors makes a significant dent in the hot water bill at this mountainside resort.

Solar Ovens

Solar ovens and cookers are simple devices that capture heat from the sun with a reflective surface that's angled or curved toward a cooking pot. Because they can be made easily from cheap materials such as scrap cardboard and tinfoil, they are widely used in areas of the world where trees and fossil fuel are scarce or expensive. Once made, they can be used to cook food and boil water in a reasonable amount of time for absolutely no cost.

There are dozens of possible designs (see Resources, page 186); some angle the rays down into a small center area, while others focus the rays upward toward the underside of a pot, like a reversed magnifying glass. You can also buy portable solar ovens assembled from polished metal online—they're great equipment for camping. But if you're serious about integrating free fuel from the sun into your cooking, any of the three following projects is a great place to start. They work beautifully, and you can build them for a fraction of the cost of a purchased solar cooker.

Depending on variables such as location, ambient air temperature, and the angle of the sun, a solar oven can reach temperatures above boiling (212° F). In ideal conditions, some types can reach 300° or more. This temperature range is high enough that you can safely cook any food, including meat. Cooking times are longer, but because the temperature is lower there's little danger of overcooking, and the food is delicious. Parabolic cookers can reach much higher temperatures than ovens and are best suited for frying foods or boiling liquids.

Solar Oven

There are numerous ways to make a solar cooker—one website devoted to the subject has dozens of photos of different types sent in by people from all around the world—and all of them seem to work reasonably well. We settled on this model mostly because we're carpenters and we like working with wood more than metal. Feel free to modify it as you wish.

The cooker is big enough to hold two medium-size pots. All the pieces are cut from one eight-foot-long 2 × 12 and a sheet of ¾-inch plywood. The cooker would work just as well with ¼-inch plywood, but we used ¾-inch because

it made it simpler to screw the corners and edges together. The base is made from 1½-inch-thick lumber for ease of construction and for the insulation value of the thicker wood, but thinner material would also work.

The foil we used was a type recommended for durability and resistance to UV degradation by an independent research institute. Unfortunately, it was expensive, and if you're just starting out you may want to do a trial run with heavy-duty aluminum foil. Although foil looks a little dull, it actually reflects solar rays almost as well as specially polished mirrors.

TOOLS & MATERIALS

Straightedge
Circular saw
Jigsaw or plunge router
Tape measure
Drill/driver with bits
Triangle square
Stapler
Eye and ear protection

#8 countersink bit
¾" × 4 × 8' BC or better plywood
2 × 12 × 8' SPF SolaReflex foil
   (see Resources, page 186) or heavy-
   duty aluminum foil
Deck screws (1⅝, 2½")
Clear silicone caulk
Mid-size black metal pot with glass top

Contact cement, or white glue and brush,
   optional
Wire rack
¼ × 17¼ × 17¼" tempered glass
No-bore glass lid pulls (Rockler item no. 29132)
¼ × 2" hanger bolts with large fender washers
   and wingnuts
Work gloves

CUTTING LIST

KEY	NUMBER	DIMENSION	PART	MATERIAL
A	2	1½ × 11¼ × 19"	Base	SPF
B	2	1½ × 11¼ × 16"	Base	SPF
C	1	¾ × 19 × 19"	Bottom	Plywood
D	1	¾ × 10 × 17"	Adjustable leg	Plywood
E	1	¾ × 20 × 33¾"	Back	Plywood
F	1	¾ × 10 × 25¼"	Front	Plywood
G	2	¾ × 20 × 31¼"	Sides	Plywood
H	1	¼ × 17¼ × 17¼"	Cover	Tempered glass

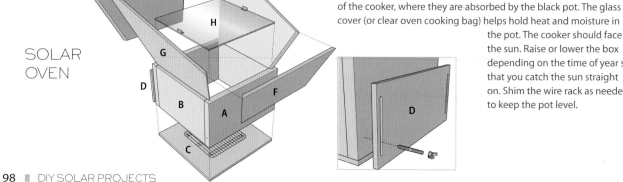

SOLAR
OVEN

Sun rays reflect off the foil sides and are concentrated at the base of the cooker, where they are absorbed by the black pot. The glass cover (or clear oven cooking bag) helps hold heat and moisture in the pot. The cooker should face the sun. Raise or lower the box depending on the time of year so that you catch the sun straight on. Shim the wire rack as needed to keep the pot level.

How to Build a Solar Oven

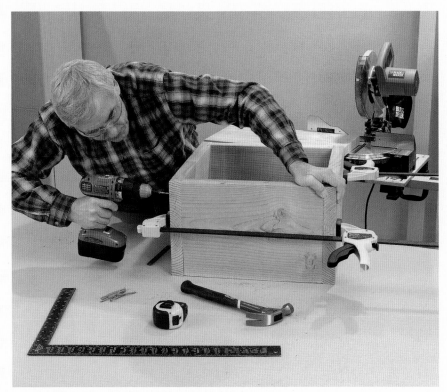

1 Cut the four 2 × 12 base pieces to length according to the cutting list. Arrange the base parts on a flat work surface and clamp them together in the correct orientation. Check with a carpenter's square and adjust the parts as needed. Then drill pilot holes and fasten the pieces together with 2½" deck screws.

2 Lay a 4 × 8' sheet of plywood on the worksurface with the better side facing up. Select a good grade of ¾" plywood (we used BC) or you're likely to have issues with parts warping, and you'll find it difficult to drive screws into the edge grain of the plywood. Mark and cut the 19 × 19" bottom piece first. Rest the full sheet of plywood on a couple of old 2 × 4s—you can cut through them as you make your cuts without any need to move them out of the way.

continued on page 100

3 To create the panels that form the reflector you'll need to make beveled cuts on the bottom and sides so the panels fit together squarely. With the best side of the plywood facing up, mark two 20 × 76"-long pieces, measuring from the two factory edges so the waste will be in the middle. Set your circular saw base to 22½°, then cut along the line you drew at 20" (20" is the long side of the bevel). Cut the other piece starting from the opposite end of the plywood. You should end up with two mirror image pieces.

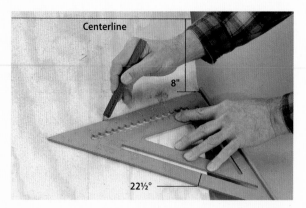

4 Re-set your saw base so it's flat, then cut each 20"-wide panel in half so you have four 20 × 38" panels, each with one beveled 38" edge. With the beveled edge facing up and closest to you, draw a centerline at 18" on each panel, then make marks on the beveled edges at 8" on both sides of the centerline. Position a triangle square so it pivots at the 8" mark, then rotate the triangle square away from the centerline until the 22½° mark on the triangle square meets the top of the beveled edge. Draw a line along the triangle square as shown, then use a straightedge to extend the line to the other edge (the factory edge) of the plywood. Repeat at the other 8" mark, flipping the triangle square and rotating it away from the centerline so the lines create a flat-topped triangle. Set the base of your circular saw at 40°, then cut along the angled lines (although it seems incorrect, 40° is the angle required to form a square corner when the pieces are assembled). Mark and cut the remaining three panels in the same fashion.

Compound Miter Corner Cuts

The sides of this solar cooker box are cut with the same basic technique used to cut crown molding. Instead of angling the crown against the miter saw fence in the same position it will be against the ceiling—a simple 45° cut that is easy to visualize—you have to make the compound cuts with the wood lying flat, which makes it mind-bendingly difficult to visualize the cut angles. For the dimensions of this cooker, a 40° bevel cut along the 22½° line will form a square corner. If you change the 22½° angle, the saw cut will also change.

If you remember your geometry you can work all this out on paper, but bevel guides on circular saws are not very precise, and 40° on one saw might be more like 39° on a different brand; test cuts are the best way to get the angle right. Make the first cuts a little long and then try them out.

The easiest way to avoid a miscut is to lay all the pieces out with the bases lined up and the good side of the plywood up. Mark the 22½° lines for the sides, then cut the 40° angles on one edge of all four pieces. Next, flip the piece around and cut the 40° angle on the other side. Remember, the 40° cut should angle outwards from the good side of the plywood, and the pieces should all be mirror images.

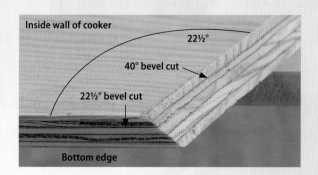

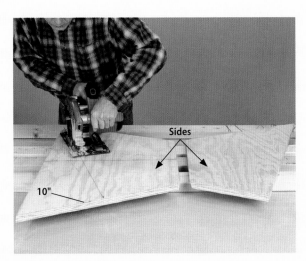

5 Finish cutting the reflector parts to final size and shape. *TIP: Clamping or holding smaller parts for cutting can be tricky. Here is a useful trick: After you've laid out your cutting lines, set the workpiece onto a pair of old 2 × 4s. Tack the workpieces to the 2 × 4s with finish nails, ideally driven into the waste area of the panels. Keep the nails at least a couple of inches from any cutting line. Set your saw so the cutting depth is about ¼" more than the thickness of the workpiece and then make your cuts.*

6 Assemble the reflector. Brace two of the reflector sides against a square piece of scrap plywood clamped to the work surface, then join the edges with screws driven into countersunk pilot holes. Repeat for the other two pieces, then join the two halves together with four screws at each corner, completing the reflector. The bottom edges should be aligned. The top edges won't match perfectly, so sand them smooth.

7 Make the adjustable leg, which contains parallel slots so the leg can move up and down over a pair of hanger bolts, raising and lowering the angle of the cooker so you can take full advantage of the direction of the sun's rays. Outline the slots in the adjustable leg of the oven so they are ⅜" wide (or slightly wider than your hanger bolt shafts). Locate a slot 2" from each edge of the adjustable leg. The slots should stop and start 2" from the top and bottom edges. Cut the slots with a jigsaw or a plunge router.

8 Screw the base and the plywood bottom together. Set the adjustable leg against one side of the base, then drill guide holes and install the hanger bolts so they will align with the slots. The centers of the bolts should be at the same height: roughly 2½" up from the bottom of the box. Use large fender washers and wingnuts to lock the adjustable leg in position.

continued on page 102

9 Fasten the reflector to the base with countersunk 2½" screws. Angle the drill bit slightly as you drill to avoid breaking the plywood edge. Use two screws per side.

10 Cut pieces of reflective sheeting to fit the sides of the reflector as well as the base. You can use heavy-duty aluminum foil, but for a sturdier option try solar foil (see Resources, page 186). The product seen here is essentially polyethylene tarp material with a reflective aluminum surface. Make sure to cut the pieces large enough so they overlap the edges and can be easily attached.

11 Glue the reflective sheeting inside the base and reflector, overlapping the corners so all bare wood is covered. Use contact cement or silicone caulk to adhere solar foil, and staple the edges to reinforce the glue; use diluted white glue with a paint brush instead of contact cement if you're using aluminum foil. Pull or smooth out the reflective material as much as possible; the smoother the surface is, the better it will reflect light.

12 Take measurements to double-check the glass lid size. Ideally, the lid will fit in so it comes to rest about 1" above the top opening of the box. As shown here, a ¼ × 17 × 17" piece of tempered glass fits just right. Be sure to order glass with polished edges. You can also just use a clear plastic oven bag instead of the glass. Either will trap heat and speed up the cooking.

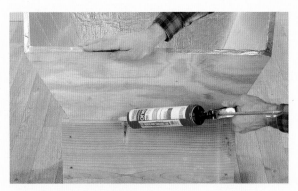

13 Caulk the joint between the angled top and the base with clear, 100% silicone caulk. Set a wire rack inside the oven to keep the cooking pot slightly elevated and allow airflow beneath it.

Handling Solar Materials

If you use rugged solar foil to create the reflective surface, you can glue it to the 2 × 12s and the plywood base prior to assembly. If you are using heavy-duty aluminum foil, which tears easily, you'll get better results if you glue it to the wood surfaces after the box is assembled.

Getting a Handle on Glass

Since it is virtually impossible to lift the glass lid from above, you'll need to install handles or pulls designed to attach to glass (available from woodworking hardware suppliers) to lift and replace the glass cover. The simplest of these (see Resources, page 186) require no drilling. You squeeze a bead of clear, 100% silicone into the U-channel of the lid handle, then slide the handle over the edge of the glass.

Cooking with a Solar Cooker

Anything that can be cooked in a slow cooker, including meat, can be cooked in a solar cooker (as long as the

sun is out!). You can also make bread and other baked goods, rice, fish, potatoes, and dozens of other dishes. You'll need to experiment a little with a cooking thermometer, because cooking times will vary depending on the time of year and where you live; most foods will need two to four hours. Other points to keep in mind when cooking in a solar oven:

- Be sure to adjust the back leg so there are no shadows in the cooker, and move the cooker every hour or so to face the sun directly.

- Since the cooking temperature is fairly low and the food is in a closed pot, it won't overcook or dry out if you leave it in too long.

- You can use a candy thermometer or oven thermometer to find out how hot the oven is. This will help you determine cooking time.

- Avoid opening the lid unless absolutely necessary—it's estimated that every time you open the lid you add 15 minutes to the cooking time.

- Wipe down the interior of the oven after every usage. Keeping the glass lid clean allows as much sunlight in as possible.

- You cannot cook in the oven without a dark pot with a lid. The dark metal of the pot is warmed by the sunlight and transfers its heat to the food.

- See the Resources section (page 186) for links to sites with solar cooking recipes.

- Do not allow children to use the solar oven unless they are under direct adult supervision.

Portable Solar Oven

This oven is a lightweight, semi-collapsible version of the wood solar oven on pages 97 to 103. The sides and bottom of this version are made with rigid foam insulation board, which is lightweight and helps retain heat. The reflector panels are made of corrugated plastic covered with silver Mylar sheeting for maximum reflectivity. The four panels slip into grooves cut into wood channels along the top of the oven box, so you can easily pull them out and stack them together for compact storage or transport.

Another handy feature is the swinging rack inside the oven box. Made with a wire cooling rack suspended by a hanger wire on each side, the rack pivots when the oven is tilted to follow the sun, keeping the cooking vessel level at all times. Simply tilt the oven box to the desired angle, and prop it up with a couple of bricks or scrap wood. The rack adjusts itself by force of gravity.

TOOLS & MATERIALS

Tape measure	4 × 8' sheet of 1½" polyisocyanurate insulation board	10 × 10" heavy wire cooling rack
Utility knife		(2) 1½" wood screws
Yardstick	Foamboard construction adhesive	¼ × ¼ × 76" high-temperature foam gasket tape
Caulk gun	Duct tape	
Clamps	2 × 2 board, 8' long	¼" plate glass, 17¼ × 17¼"
Circular saw	4 × 8' sheet of 0.157" (4 mm) corrugated plastic	100-grit sandpaper
Miter saw		(2) ⅜" offset window screen clips with screws
Protractor	Foamboard adhesive	
Fine-tip marker	Black spray adhesive	(2) Metal door pulls designed for glass doors
Utility knife	2-mil silver Mylar, 4 × 6' (or 20" × 12')	
Scissors	¾"-wide hook-and-loop tape, 3'	Eye and ear protection
Needlenose pliers	14-ga. steel wire, 56" min.	Work gloves

CUTTING LIST

KEY	NUMBER	DIMENSION	PART	MATERIAL
A	2	1½ × 12 × 19"	Box side	1½" foam insulation board
B	2	1½ × 12 × 16"	Box side	1½" foam insulation board
C	1	1½ × 19 × 19"	Box bottom	1½" foam insulation board
D	4	1½ × 1½ × 19"	Channel	2 × 2 lumber
E	4	0.157 × 20¾ × 17½"	Reflector panel	Corrugated plastic
F	4	2 mils × cut to fit	Mylar	Mylar sheeting
G	1	¼ × 17 × 17"	Cover	Glass
H	1	¼ × 17¼ × 17¼"	Cover	Tempered glass

PORTABLE SOLAR OVEN

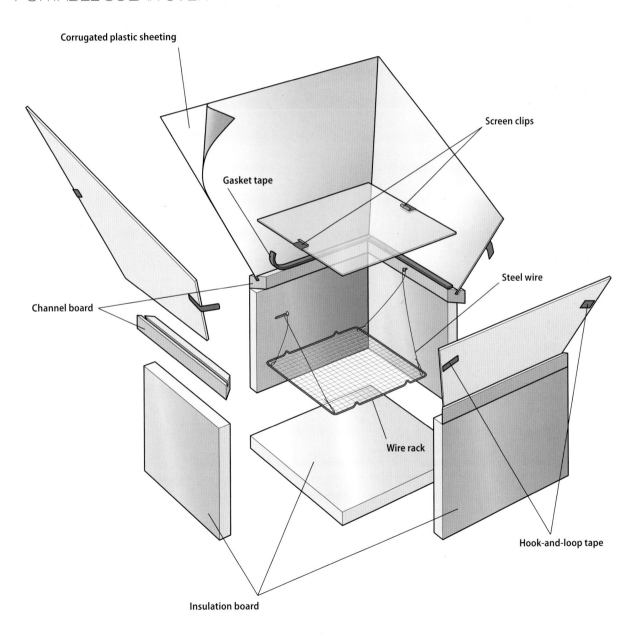

Corrugated plastic sheeting

Screen clips

Gasket tape

Channel board

Steel wire

Wire rack

Hook-and-loop tape

Insulation board

How to Build a Portable Solar Oven

1 Build the box by cutting two pieces of insulation board to size at 12 × 19" and two pieces at 12 × 16" for the four sides, using a utility knife and a yardstick. Cut one piece at 19 × 19" for the bottom. Glue the sides together over the bottom with foamboard adhesive to form a 19" square. Tape the pieces in place, and let the adhesive cure as directed. *NOTE: Any insulation board you use must be rated for temperatures higher than 450°F.*

2 Create the top channel by clamping an 8' 2 × 2 to a work surface and drawing a centerline down the length of the board. Set a circular saw to cut a 22½° bevel at a depth of ¾". Cut along the line, moving the clamps if necessary, to cut at least 78" of channel. Test-fit a piece of corrugated plastic sheeting in the channel; it should slide in easily for a snug fit. If necessary, widen the channel as needed by making a second pass with the saw.

3 Complete the box by cutting four pieces of 2 × 2 channel to length at 19", mitering the ends at 45°. Glue the pieces to the top edges of the box sides with foamboard adhesive so all of the beveled grooves angle outward from the box center and they meet at the corners. Let the adhesive cure, then paint the interior of the box with black spray paint.

4 Lay out the reflector panels as shown in the Panel Layout drawing (page 105), using a yardstick, protractor, and marker. All of the four panels have the same width along the bottom, and both sides are angled outward at 67.5° toward the top. Cut out the panels with a utility knife. Test-fit all four panels by inserting their bottom edges all the way into the box channel grooves, and trim any panels as needed so they meet at the corners (it's not a problem if the corners have small gaps).

5 Cut the Mylar sheeting by placing each reflector panel facedown onto the backside of the Mylar and cutting the Mylar around the panel, leaving an ample margin on all sides. Turn the panels face up and coat them with spray adhesive. Apply the Mylar to the panels so it is smooth and flat, then bend the excess over the backside of the panels and glue in place with spray adhesive.

6 Reposition the reflector panels on the oven box and align their edges at the corners. Cut 4"-long strips of hook-and-loop tape and apply one set of strips to secure the two adjacent panels together at each corner, about ⅔ of the distance up from the oven box. Apply the strips at an angle so they remain flat. Separate the strips and remove the panels for the next step.

7 Construct the swinging rack. Cut two 28" lengths of wire with needlenose pliers. Make a full loop in the wire 11¼" from the tied end, creating a small hole inside the loop. Now, loop one free end of the wire around the front corner of the metal cooling rack and twist to secure it. Secure the remaining loose end of the wire to the rear corner of the rack. Repeat on the other side of the rack. Finally, hang the rack on each side from a single 1½" screw driven on the inside side walls of the box. The screws should be ¾" down from the top edges of the side wood channels and 7" from the inside face of the rear channel.

8 Apply high-temperature gasket tape or weatherseal to the top edges of the 2 × 2. Install two offset screen clips, each centered on a side channel, at least ¼" from the inside edge of the wood, using screws.

9 Have a piece of ¼" glass cut to 17¼" square. Ask the glass supplier to sand the sharp edges, or sand them with 100-grit sandpaper. Attach metal door pulls designed for glass doors as handles for the sides of the glass. (You may need to buy these at a woodworking or cabinet supply company.) When using the cooker, use these handles to insert and remove the glass in the cooker.

Solar Parabolic Cooker

A solar parabolic, or dish, cooker is a relatively high-powered tool for cooking or heating food with the sun. In full sun, even a moderately sized dish can smolder cardboard in a minute or two and ignite it in under three minutes. Properly constructed and used, it can boil water or fry food. Parabolic dishes also make great experiment and demonstration projects for students or anyone interested in learning how to harness the sun's power.

A parabolic solar cooker works in somewhat the same way as a magnifying glass: it focuses light on a single point, which in this case is the cooking area suspended above the center of the dish. The shape of the dish always reflects the light to the same point, so you don't have to adjust the focus like you do with a magnifying glass. Of course, the dish must face the sun for maximum heat, so you may have to move the dish if you're cooking for long periods.

The amount of heat energy created by a parabolic cooker is based on the size of the dish and the reflectivity of its surface. A larger, shinier (and smoother) surface creates more heat than a smaller dish with a duller surface. On the other hand, smaller cookers are lighter and more portable. The cooker in this project is moderately sized and is lightweight but sturdy. Its dish is 36 inches in diameter and has a reflective surface of silver Mylar backed by corrugated plastic panels. The panels are supported by ribs made of 1½-inch-thick rigid foam insulation cut with the parabolic shape. The ribs are mounted to a ½-inch plywood base, and the dish is surrounded by a 1× lumber border to protect the ribs and make the unit easy to store.

TOOLS & MATERIALS

Tape measure
Circular saw
Jigsaw with fine-tooth wood blade
    and metal-cutting blade
4' level or straightedge
Protractor
Drill with pilot bits and twist bit set
Caulk gun
Scissors
Fine marker
Utility knife
Hacksaw
Triangle square
(3 to 4) 2-lb. bags of sand or similar material

Pipe wrench
½" plywood, 4 × 4' sheet (37½" × 37½" min.)
Scrap 2× lumber (3 × 3" min.)
(2) 1 × 8 boards, 8-ft. long
Construction adhesive
¾" and 1½" screws
Poster board
1½"-thick rigid polyisocyanurate foam
    insulation board
Corrugated plastic, 5⁄16" × 24" × 72"
Spray adhesive
5⁄16" threaded rod, 22" min.
5⁄16" nuts and washers (2 each)
(2) 1½" × 4" (or similar) tie plates

2 × 2 board, 8' long
1½" × 6" strap hinges
(2) Screw hooks
Galvanized metal chain, 8½ linear feet
¾" threaded black steel or galvanized
    pipe (two 18", one 20", one 42")
¾" steel side outlet elbow
¾" steel 90° elbow
(3) ¾" steel pipe caps
S-hook for ¾" pipe
(4) S-hooks for chain
9-ga. expanded metal (14 × 14")
Eye and ear protection
Work gloves

CUTTING LIST

KEY	NUMBER	DIMENSION	PART	MATERIAL
A	1	½ × 37½ × 37½"	Base bottom	Plywood
B	1	1½ × 1½ × 3"	Center block	2-by lumber
C	2	¾ × 7¼ × 36"	Base side	1 × 8 lumber
D	2	¾ × 7¼ × 37½"	Base side	1 × 8 lumber
E	1	6 × 16½"	Rib template	Poster board
F	8	1½ × 6 × 16½"	Rib (full-length)	1½" foam insulation board
G	8	1½ × 6 × 15"	Rib (trimmed)	1½" foam insulation board
H	1	7 × 18½"	Dish panel template	Poster board
I	16	5/16 × 7 × 18½"	Dish panel	Corrugated plastic
J	1	2 mils × cut to fit	Mylar	Mylar sheeting
K	1	5/16 × 22"	Threaded rod	5/16" threaded rod
L	2	1½ × 1½ × 22"	Leg	2 × 2 lumber
M	2	1½ × 1½ × 17"	Cross piece	2 × 2 lumber
N	1	30"	Chain (for legs)	Galvanized chain
O	1	14 × 14"	Metal square (pot support)	Expanded metal
P	4	16"	Chain (for metal square pot support)	Galvanized chain

SOLAR PARABOLIC COOKER

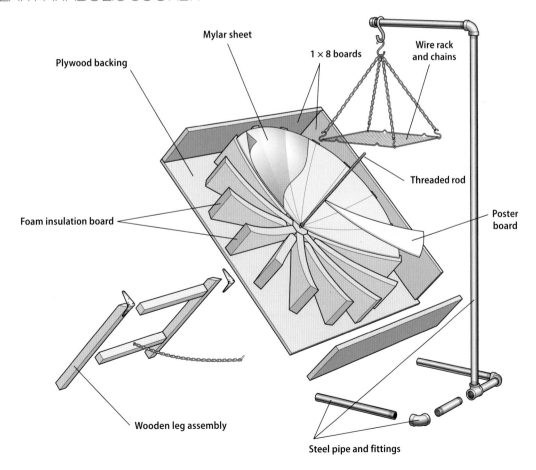

Plywood backing

Mylar sheet

1 × 8 boards

Wire rack and chains

Threaded rod

Poster board

Foam insulation board

Wooden leg assembly

Steel pipe and fittings

☀ How to Build a Solar Parabolic Cooker

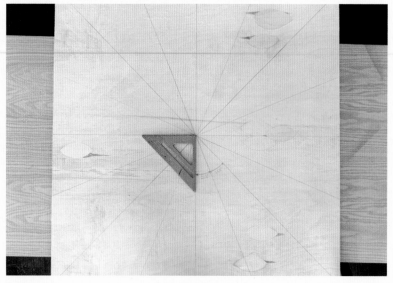

1 Cut a 37½" × 37½" square of ½" plywood using a circular saw or jigsaw. Mark the square's center by using a level or straightedge to draw two diagonal lines from corner to corner; the center is where the lines intersect. Measure and mark the center of each of the four sides, then connect these marks across the center point to create a horizontal and vertical axis, dividing the square into eight sections. Position a triangle square or protractor at the center of the square and mark 22½° angles, then draw lines through these marks and the center point to bisect the eight original sections. There are now a total of 16 sections.

2 Flip the plywood base over and draw horizontal and vertical axis lines on the backside. (You will use these lines later to position the leg assembly.) Drill a ⁵⁄₁₆" hole through the center point of the plywood base for installing the threaded guide rod later.

3 Create the octagonal center block by cutting a 3" square of scrap 2× lumber (1½" thick). Mark the center point by drawing diagonals, then draw a horizontal-vertical axis, as with the plywood base. Make a mark ⁵⁄₈" to both sides of the axis lines, then connect these marks to draw an octagon. Cut off the four triangular corners along these lines. Drill a ⁵⁄₁₆" hole through the center point to complete the block.

4 Cut two pieces of 1" × 8' to length at 36" and two pieces at 37½". Apply construction adhesive to the bottom edges, and glue the boards along the edges of the top face of the plywood base, so the longer pieces cover the ends of the shorter pieces. Drill pilot holes, and screw the boards together at the corners, using 1½" screws. Also fasten the boards with screws driven through the bottom of the base.

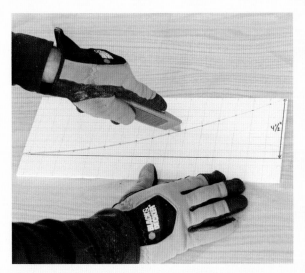

5 Create a rib template on poster board, enlarging the template to a full-size grid, as shown. The curve starts with a ½" increment because the first 1½" of the parabola is essentially flat (horizontal) and will be taken up by the octagonal center block. Lay out the curve by making a mark at each vertical line, using the dimensions given. Connect the marks with a smooth, curving line to draw the parabola. Cut out the poster board template with scissors or a utility knife.

6 Trace around the template to draw 16 ribs onto 1½" rigid insulation board, using a fine marker. Cut out the ribs with a jigsaw.

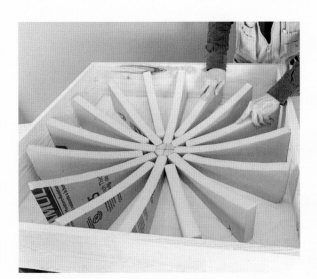

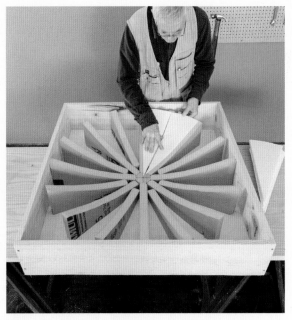

7 Glue the center block to the center of the plywood base, using construction adhesive. Glue eight ribs to the base along every other layout line, so they are centered over the layout lines with the short ends butted against a facet of the center block. The tops of the ribs should be flush with the top of the block. Because of the thickness of the foam board, the final eight ribs cannot fit against the center block, and will need to be shorter; trim off 1½" at the front of the ribs to make them fit, then glue into place between the full length ribs.

8 Draw a panel template onto poster board as shown. It is a conical shape with 18½" sides and a 7"-wide base. Cut out the panel template, then test fit it on several pairs of ribs, centering the panel on both ribs. Trim the template as needed for a good fit.

continued on page 112

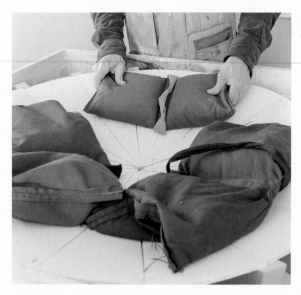

9 Trace 16 panels onto corrugated plastic, making sure the long sides of the panels are perpendicular to the ribs of the corrugation. Cut out the pieces with a utility knife. Apply thin, wavy beads of construction adhesive to the ribs and apply the panels to the ribs, pressing them down to follow the rib curve. Weigh down the panels with bags of sand, rice, or similar material until the adhesive has set.

10 Spray the dish surface with spray adhesive, then carefully lay a sheet of Mylar over the dish. Smooth the center area down, then work outward, spraying and smoothing as you go. Your goal is the smoothest possible reflective surface. Trim away the excess Mylar.

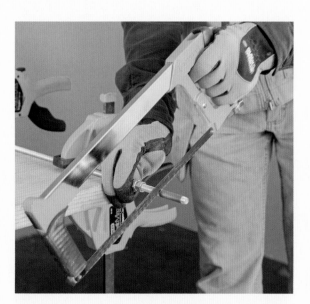

11 Mark a length of ⁵⁄₁₆" threaded rod at 22". Thread two nuts onto the rod so they are about 18" from one end and both inside of the 22" mark. Cut the rod at the mark, using a hacksaw. Place a washer over the rod end, and insert it through the hole in the dish's center block, so the rod projects up out of the bottom of the reflective dish. Secure the rod on the backside of the plywood base with another washer and nut.

12 Construct the leg assembly by cutting two 2" × 2" legs to length at 22", mitering the top ends at 45°. Cut two cross pieces at 17". Position the cross pieces between the legs, 3" from the ends of the legs. Drill countersunk pilot holes and join the pieces with two screws.

13 Attach a strap hinge to the mitered top of each leg, opposite the bevel, using the provided screws. Mount the hinges to the plywood base so the leg assembly is centered over the vertical layout line and is 3" up from the horizontal line. Install a screw hook into the plywood base, positioned on the vertical line and 14" down from the horizontal line. Install another screw hook into the top face of the lower crosspiece, centered between the legs. Cut a 30" length of metal chain, using a hacksaw. Attach the chain to the screw hooks; this will secure the legs in place when the dish is tilted in position for use.

14 Assemble the cooking stand with prethreaded steel pipe and fittings. Thread two 18" pipes into the two side outlets of a 3-way fitting to form the stand base. Tighten the connections with a pipe wrench. Add caps to the ends of the pipes. Thread a 42" pipe into the top outlet of the 3-way, extending up. Add a 90° elbow to the top vertical pipe and then a 20" pipe outward from the elbow. Slip an S-hook onto the 20" pipe, then add a cap.

15 Cut a 14" square of expanded metal using a jigsaw and metal-cutting blade. Use small S-hooks and four 16" lengths of chain to hang the metal square from a single S-hook in the center, then hang the assembly to the large S-hook on the stand with a 12" length of chain. *TIP: You can substitute a heavy-duty wire cooling rack for the expanded metal. Choose a size of rack that you won't have to cut down.*

Setting Up Your Cooker

Position the cooker dish so it is perpendicular to the sun, adjusting the legs so they are roughly perpendicular to the dish's base. Secure the legs in position with the chain. The focal point of the reflected sunlight should be at the end of the threaded rod. If necessary, adjust the rod in or out by moving the nuts so that the focal point is at the end of the rod. You should have to do this only once, as the focal point does not change with the dish's angle.

Position the cooking stand and adjust the height of the cooking basket so the expanded metal plate is on the focal point, as marked by the end of the threaded rod. Place your cooking pan or pot onto the metal plate, and start cookin'!

A few tips for best results:

• Use a dark-colored pan or skillet for cooking; cast iron is ideal because it is dark and heats relatively evenly.

• Rotate the pan frequently for even heating.

• Adjust the dish's position to maintain maximum heat if the cooking lasts more than 10 minutes.

Solar Water Heater

The basic principle of a solar water heater is simple. Water or an antifreeze solution flows through pipes in a large, flat, enclosed box known as a flat plate collector, or through a series of vacuum tubes in an array known as an evacuated-tube collector. As the liquid moves through the system, solar heat is transferred to it. In a thermosyphon system, the solar-heated water flows into a storage tank and is used directly. In a drainback system, the solar-heated liquid—which can be water or antifreeze solution—flows into a heat exchanger inside a water-storage tank, where it heats potable water; the solar-heated liquid is not used directly.

Storing the hot water in a separate tank is necessary because it takes longer for the water to heat up, and because a large supply is needed to last through the night and early morning. Solar water heaters are usually paired with a conventional gas or electric water heater—either a tank or a tankless, point-of-use type—to ensure uninterrupted hot water during cloudy periods or times of heavy use, but the conventional heater won't turn on unless it's needed, which saves considerable money. And solar hot water heaters work anytime the sun is out, even in winter.

A number of different manufactured hot water collectors are available, but you can build your own for a fraction of the cost using wood, copper pipe, and polycarbonate glazing—all materials available at home centers. The concept is simple, and can be modified to fit your house and needs. There are also many alternative designs available on the internet (see Resources, page 186).

Solar hot-water collectors can serve a number of different purposes. If you have enough sun, they can provide all the hot water for your household, but even on cloudy days the water will warm up enough to reduce the amount of energy you need. Using them with tankless heaters saves even more money, eliminating the need to keep a conventional water tank full of expensively heated water all day and night. Hot water collectors can also be used to provide heat for pools and hot tubs, and to heat water for use in a heating system.

This attractive solar heater array provides hot water for two families.

If you can solder pipe and cut wood, you can build a collector like this, and start saving money on water heating costs right away.

Copper Tubing Heater Panel

This flat plate collector can be used with several different types of solar hot water systems. In warm climates it can work with a thermosyphon storage tank (see page 128); in cooler climates where freezing is a problem it can be used as a rooftop or wall collector with a drainback system (see page 130) or other type of pump-controlled system. It's also possible to use this collector with a system containing antifreeze, but water heaters with antifreeze require special plumbing and safety features to avoid contaminating the water supply, and should be discussed with a plumbing inspector or left to an expert.

The collector is constructed of wood with a layer of insulation to help retain heat. The panel covering it is made from polycarbonate, a type of clear acrylic that resists the UV damage that clouds and cracks regular acrylic. Cool water comes in through a ¾-inch pipe at the bottom and is gradually heated as it rises through a manifold of ½-inch copper pipes. Heat is collected and transferred to the pipes by thin aluminum panels lining the box and shaped over the copper. As the water warms in the pipes, it rises to the top and flows into the upper part of the storage tank as cool water from the bottom of the storage tank flows in to replace it. This water movement continues until the water

in the storage tank is hotter than the water in the collector, at which point the thermosyphon action stops or the thermostatically-controlled pump switches off.

The collector can be mounted on the ground (as we did—see page 126), the roof, or the side of the building, at an angle based on the latitude (see page 125). However, these collectors can get quite hot during the summer months, and they are often placed at a steeper angle so that they face the low winter sun more directly, and deflect some of the intense heat from the high summer sun.

Use polyisocyanurate rigid insulation (usually called "polyiso") for the insulation in a solar collector as it has the highest R-value and is also the most heat-resistant type of rigid insulation. Polyiso has a variety of trade names; just look for the insulation with the highest R-value.

To simplify construction, the size of this collector is based on a sheet of plywood, but it can be built a different size or orientation or ganged together with other collectors to make a larger array. Deciding how big a collector you need is mostly trial and error based on your usage and climate, but the square footage of a sheet of plywood is a good starting point for an average household. If it's not enough, you can always add another one.

TOOLS & MATERIALS

Level	¾ × 1½" top nailer for glazing	½ × 85½" Type L copper
Circular saw	½ × 49½" EMT cross supports for glazing	¾ copper tubing cut to fit
Miter saw	Neoprene rubber screws	(pieces between Ts)
Tape measure	Deck screws (1¼", 1⅝", 2½")	(2) 10" long × ¾"
Drill/driver with bits	¾" machine screws	(inlet and outlet)
Stapler	½" machine screws	(2) ¾ × ¾ PEX adapters
Razor knife	6d galvanized casing nails	¾" PEX tubing
Soldering torch	Aluminum soffit panels	(to inside house)
Wire brush for copper pipe	Aluminum coil stock	¾" pipe wrap insulation
Adjustable wrenches	Paintable acrylic caulk	Lead-free solder
Hammer	Clear silicone caulk	Paste flux
½" plywood	Polycarbonate glazing	Teflon tape
½" × 4' × 8' plywood	(¼" × 2 × 8' panels)	Copper pipe straps
¾" rigid polyisocyanurate insulation	Closure strips	EMT conduits
¼" plywood 2 × 4 × 8' for sides,	(sold with glazing)	½ and ¾" type L copper tubing
bottom 2 × 6 × 51" for top	Stainless-steel staples	Copper fittings
Copper tubing cutter	Emery cloth	Hose bibb
Sledgehammer	¾ × ½" Ts	PEX tubing
⅝" steel rod	¾ × ¾" T	PEX to copper transitions
High-temperature black paint	¾ × ½" elbows	Copper-soldering supplies
PEX crimping tool	¾" elbow	¾" pipe wrap insulation
¾ × ¾" inside nailers,	¾" male threaded coupling	Eye and ear protection
nailers for glazing, caps for top	¾" cap	Work gloves
and bottom	¾" hose bibb	

SOLAR HOT WATER COLLECTOR

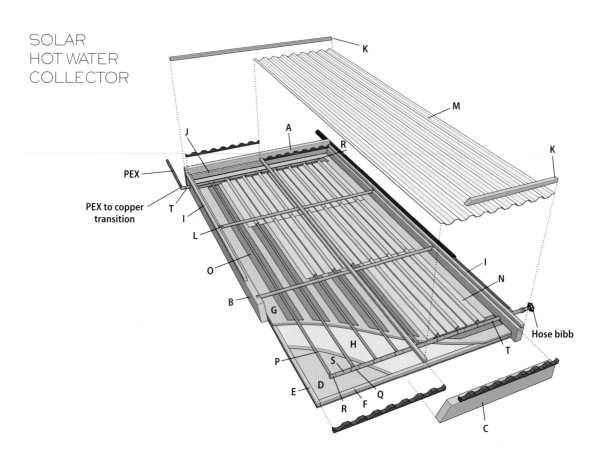

PEX

PEX to copper transition

Hose bibb

CUTTING LIST

KEY	NUMBER	DIMENSION	PART	MATERIAL
A	1	1½" × 5½" × 48"	Top	PT or SPF
B	2	1½" × 3½" × 95"	Sides	SPF
C	1	1½" × 3½" × 45"	Bottom	SPF
D	1	¼" × 45" × 93½"	Underside	Plywood
E	2	¾" × ¾" × 93½"	Nailers	Pine
F	2	¾" × ¾" × 43½"	Nailers	Pine
G	1	½" × 45" × 93½"	Collector panel	Plywood
H	1	¾" × 43½" × 92"	Insulation	Polyiso
I	3	¾" × ¾" × 95"	Nailers	Pine
J	1	¾" × 1½" × 45"	Upper nailer	Pine
K	2	¾" × ¾" × 48"	Caps	Cedar or PT
L	2	½" × 46½"	Glazing supports	EMT
M	2	¼" × 2' × 8'	Glazing	Polycarbonate
N	24	28" × 6¾"	Heat collectors	Aluminum soffit panels
O	8	4" × 84"	Heat collectors	Aluminum coil stock
P	8	½" × 85½"	Long tube	Type L copper
Q	14	½" to ¾"	Tee	Copper fitting
R	2	½" to ¾"	Elbow	Copper fitting
S	14	¾" × cut to fit	Connector	Type L copper
T	8	¾" × cut to fit	In/out pipe	Type L copper

How to Build a Copper Tubing Heater Panel

1 The frame that houses this solar water heater is constructed from 2" × 4" and 2" × 6" dimensional lumber. Cut the pieces of the frame to length, then join them with 2½" deck screws driven into pilot holes.

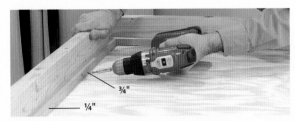

2 Cut the ¼" plywood to size, then set it inside the frame as a spacer for the ¾" × ¾" nailers. If you can't locate ¾" × ¾" trim stock for the nailers at your building center, rip-cut ¾"-thick strips from a piece of 1× stock (a tablesaw is best for this, but you can use a circular saw and straightedge cutting guide, too). Screw the nailers to the inner perimeter of the frame with 1⅝" deck screws. Check to make sure the plywood is flush in back as you fasten the nailers.

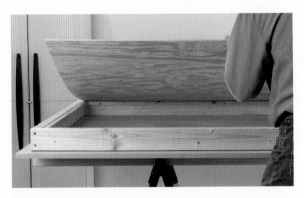

3 Flip the frame over and set the ¼" plywood back into the frame against the nailers. Screw the plywood in place with ¾" machine screws driven through the back panel into the nailers.

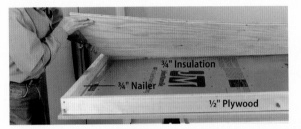

4 Cut panels of ¾"-thick closed-cell, foil-faced polyiso insulation and fit them inside the frame between the ¾" nailers, flush with the tops of the nailers. Cut a panel of ½" plywood to fit inside the frame over the insulation and the nailers and attach the plywood to the nailers, driving a 1¼" screw every 10" to 12" around the perimeter. Caulk the gap between the ½" plywood and the frame with clear, 100% silicone caulk.

5 The "guts" of this solar water heater is an array of copper tubing through which the water runs to absorb heat while it resides inside the box. The matrix of copper tubes is assembled using ¾-to-½" reducing Ts connected by short lengths of ¾" tubing on the ends and long lengths of ½" tubing filling out the space from end-to-end. Making this copper "manifold" requires that you be able to solder copper plumbing pipe. Cut all the copper pieces to length, then clean, flux, and assemble them into the grid as seen in the diagram on page 118. Make the inlet and outlet pipes a few inches longer than you need—they'll be cut shorter after pressure-testing the completed manifold.

continued on page 120

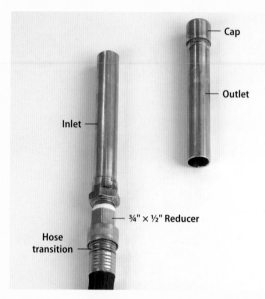

6 Solder all the pieces together. Protect the floor from drips of solder and flux with a dropcloth. Wait at least 5 minutes to touch the copper after soldering it—it will be very hot.

7 Before placing the manifold in the collector box, test the manifold for leaks. Solder a cap to the outlet at the top, then solder a ¾ × ½" reducer/male coupling to the inlet at the bottom. Wrap the threads with teflon tape, then attach the hose transition (available at home centers). Attach a hose and turn the water on. Leave it on for a few minutes; if there's a leak in one of the joints, you'll hear air and then water hissing out. If there are no leaks, drain the water and cut the cap and the reducer coupling off, then shorten both pipes to 5" measured from the last T.

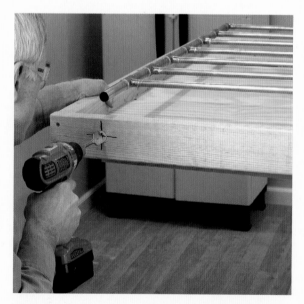

8 Mark the location of the cold-water inlet and the warm-water outlet on the sides of the box by setting the copper grid into the box and extending the inlet and outlet port locations onto the outside of the frame. Drill the holes with a 1"-diameter bit.

9 Mark the manifold locations on the plywood, then cut 4"-wide pieces of aluminum flashing and staple them so they are centered under each length of copper. These will help transfer the heat to the copper pipes. Use stainless-steel staples.

10 There are a few suppliers for preformed aluminum fins (see Resources, page 186), but you can easily make your own using aluminum soffit panels, a plywood jig, and a sledgehammer. Build a jig to make your aluminum fins using two pieces of ⅝"-thick plywood or hardwood screwed to a plywood base. Space the gap between the two plywood pieces by using the ⅝" steel rod and two scraps of aluminum soffit as a guide. Buy solid (not vented) soffit panels with V-grooves and then cut the panels using a razor knife and straight edge into 6¾"-wide strips with the V-groove in the center. The V-grooves are then formed into round channels that fit tightly over the copper pipe. Form them by pounding a ⅝"-diameter steel rod down into them with a sledgehammer (or similar heavy weight).

11 Fasten the manifold in place with copper pipe straps, equidistant from the edges. Spread a bead of silicone caulk on both sides of the copper pipe to fill the void along the bottom edge, then push the aluminum fin sections over the pipe and staple or screw them down as close as possible to the pipe. (The silicone helps to transfer heat from the fin to the copper.) Butt the fins against each other.

12 Create cross-bar supports for the polycarbonate glazing by installing two lengths of ½" EMT conduit across the box. Drill ¾" holes halfway through the 2 × 4 sides, centering the drill bit ⅜" down and drilling from the inside. Square the holes with a chisel, then place the conduit in the holes.

¾" Nailer

13 Lay the glazing on top of the box and mark the spots for ¾" nailers at the sides and the center overlap. Fasten the strips with 6d galvanized casing nails.

continued on page 122

14 Paint the entire inside of the collector with black, high-temperature paint.

Screws with neoprene washers

15 Place closure strips at the top and bottom and lay the corrugated glazing in place. Caulk the overlap between the two panels with a thin bead of clear silicone. Predrill the screw holes on the sides, then enlarge the holes in the glazing with a ¼" bit so that the glazing can move with temperature changes. Fasten the glazing with neoprene screws every foot on the sides. In the center, predrill with a smaller bit and use ½" machine screws every two feet. Squirt a dab of silicone in and around these holes before tightening the screw to seal around it.

16 Cover the ends of the glazing with ¾" wood strips. Predrill and fasten the strips with 2½" deck screws. Caulk the strip at the top against the 2 × 6 cap using paintable acrylic caulk.

17 Solder on the last copper fittings and the PEX (crosslinked polyethylene) adapters. PEX is easier to snake through the house than rigid copper. It also makes it possible to adjust the collector angle if you need to, and will flex easily if the collector moves due to soil movement or accidental bumps. Attach it to the brass PEX adapter with a brass ring and a special crimping tool. Finally, seal the inlet and outlet holes with caulk, and paint the exterior of the box. Wrap pipe insulation around the exposed copper and PEX lines, both to retain heat and to protect the PEX from UV degradation. Complete the connections inside, then fill the system (see page 137).

A Quick Guide to Soldering Copper

There's quite a bit of cutting and soldering involved in this project, and if you've never worked with copper it can seem intimidating, but as long as you follow the correct procedure and use the right tools, you'll be an expert in no time. The most important thing to remember is to test your work after you're done, so you can fix any problems before they cause real damage.

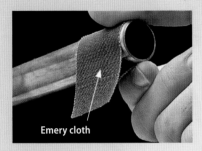

Clean the end of each pipe by sanding with emery cloth. Ends must be free of dirt and grease to ensure that the solder forms a good seal.

Clean the inside of each fitting by scouring with a wire brush or emery cloth.

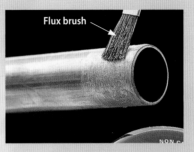

Apply a thin layer of soldering paste (flux) to the end of each pipe, using a flux brush. Soldering paste should cover about 1" of pipe end.

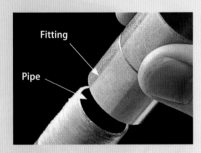

Assemble each joint by inserting the pipe into the fitting so it is tight against the bottom of the fitting sockets. Twist each fitting slightly to spread soldering paste.

Prepare the wire solder by unwinding 8" to 10" of wire from spool. Bend the first 2" of the wire to a 90º angle.

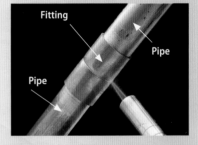

Move the torch flame back and forth and around the pipe and the fitting to heat the area evenly.

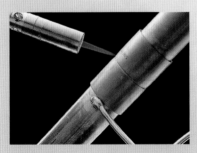

Heat the other side of the copper fitting to ensure that heat is distributed evenly. Touch solder to pipe. Solder will melt when the pipe is at the right temperature.

When solder melts, remove the torch and quickly push ½" to ¾" of solder into each joint. Capillary action fills the joint with liquid solder. A correctly soldered joint should show a thin bead of solder around the lips of the fitting.

Allow the joint to cool briefly, then wipe away excess solder with a dry rag. *CAUTION: Pipes will be hot. If joints leak after water is turned on, disassemble and resolder.*

Building a Roof or Ground Support for a Solar Collector

You can make a sturdy support for either PV panels or solar collectors by assembling lengths of Unistrut U-channel (sold at home centers and electrical suppliers; see Resources, page 186) and then anchoring them to the roof or ground. Use galvanized or stainless-steel pieces and fasteners, and follow the same guidelines for selecting a location and height.

Struts are available in several sizes, with a huge selection of accessories for joining them in dozens of configurations, though you may have to go online to find them. With a little hunting, you can usually find the right combination for almost any location or roof layout. We made ours from the basic accessories sold in the local home center, but the basic design can be put together in any number of ways with other types of fittings and fasteners.

A few considerations to keep in mind: Solar panels or hot water heaters placed on a roof need to be bolted to the rafters every 4 to 6 feet with stainless-steel or triple-galvanized lag bolts (at least $5/16 \times 4$ inches). These holes need to be waterproofed with extra care, as they will be difficult to get to once the panels are up.

Solar panel dealers carry various options for flashing roof mounts (see Resources, page 186). For shingled roofs, these are usually a bracket or holder bolted to the rafter and then covered by flashing, a rubber boot, rubber seals or some combination of these elements, with the upper part of the flashing slipped under the shingle above the holder. These mounts are the safest option when you're installing solar panels, as they've been tested and carry a manufacturer's warranty.

Build a simple, adjustable support from steel U-channel struts for either solar panels or the solar hot water collector below.

Adjustable wrench
Socket set
Metal-cutting saw
1⅝" × 10' galvanized Unistrut
    (if exterior-grade galvanized
    is unavailable, paint the metal)
½ × 1½" bolts, nuts, washers
1⅝ × 3½" Unistrut angle brackets
1⅝ × 3½" Unistrut flat
    corner brackets

⅜ × 1½" bolts
    and Unistrut
    spring-loaded nuts
Triangle Square
Hinges or L-bracket
Concrete mix
(2 or 4) Anchor bolts
Concrete pouring forms
Eye and ear protection
Work gloves

CUTTING LIST

KEY	NUMBER	DIMENSIONS	PART
A	2	80"	Base
B	2	92"	Support
C	2	36"	Back brace
D	4	20"	Brace expanders
E	4	48" (or to fit)	Cross braces

Finding the Right Angle for a Solar Collector or PV Panel

First of all, the collector should face directly south and should not be shaded, although the location doesn't have to be perfect. Crystalline solar cells should not be shaded at any part for at least six hours because shading even a small part will diminish the energy collected by the whole array, but this is not as much of a problem for thin-film solar cells or solar collectors. Solar panels and collectors are often put on roofs to elevate them above trees and shade from buildings, but they work just as well on the ground or attached to the side of a building as long as they have sufficient sunlight.

The best tilt angle is not necessarily the same for PV panels and solar collectors. For either one, though, start by finding your latitude (check online for latitude finders). The best angle for a PV panel is the same degree as your latitude, though for maximum efficiency you can move it 10° more in the winter and 10° less in the summer. For example, at latitude 45 you would

put it at 55° (from horizontal) in the winter, 45° in the spring and fall, and 35° in the summer.

For a solar collector, on the other hand, add 15° to your latitude. For example, if you live at latitude 45, the tilt angle is 60° from horizontal. Use your triangle square, which has angle markings on the outer edge, to mark this angle, then just adjust the supports for the collector until it matches the angle. This angle is generally the best for both winter and summer, because it faces the sun more directly in winter, but not as directly in summer, which lessens the chance of overheating; if you can't match it exactly, several degrees either way won't have much of an effect.

However, these are not absolute rules. Following the slope of your roof will usually be close enough to the ideal that you won't notice much difference. And it's always a good idea to talk to local dealers, installers or homeowners who have solar panels for advice about local conditions.

Angle=
latitude +10°F
(winter)
latitude −10°F
(summer)

If you're mounting the support on a sloped roof, use the triangle square to lay out the angles and determine the length of the back brace. Angles and roof pitch are both marked on the square; just align the base strut with the common rafter cut mark corresponding to your roof pitch, then align the PV support strut with the degree mark for your latitude. For example, if your roof slopes 4" in every 12" (a 4/12 pitch), the base strut will follow a line from the pivot point through the number 4 on the "Common Cuts" edge. The other strut follows the line from the pivot through the 45° mark on the outside edge.

How to Build a Roof or Ground Support for a Solar Collector

1 The easiest way to figure out the strut lengths is to lay the three pieces on the ground, move the support piece to the proper angle using the angle markings on the triangle square as a guide, then mark the cuts. Use tape to mark the location of the solar collector or panels and the points where the adjustable support leg will be attached.

2 Cut the pieces to length. Cut the cross supports to match the width of the solar collector or the length between mounting points on the PV panels.

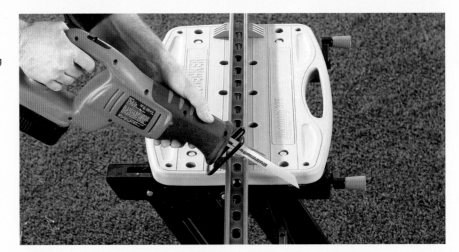

3 Cut two additional pieces of strut to 4" less than the length of the expandable brace. Cut the expandable brace in half, then bolt both halves to the long center leg with four bolts. To expand the brace to the fall or winter position, just remove the bolts on one side, push the frame up, and then bolt the pieces back together. *NOTE: Solar collectors usually stay in a fixed position year round, while PV panels benefit from being moved to summer and winter positions.*

4 Bolt the brackets and struts together, but don't join the two sides yet. Join the pieces at the base with hinges, or just use an L-bracket with a bolt as the pivot, as we did.

5 Although the PV mount is stable, it needs to be securely anchored to the ground in case of high winds. For larger arrays such as ours, add concrete footings at each corner.

Thermosyphon water heaters are the simplest type of solar water heating system; they don't require pumps or controls to move the hot water and can be used to heat house water directly, without a heat exchanger. However, they do require a storage tank, both to collect and store heated water and to keep it flowing through the collector. If house water were run through the heater without an intermediate storage tank it would either stagnate and get too hot when it wasn't being used, or flow through too quickly to get hot—like a hose lying in the sun.

The syphoning action that circulates the water starts when water in the copper pipes slowly warms up, becomes lighter (hot water weighs less than cold water), and rises through the collecter and then uphill to the top of the storage tank. As the water rises it pulls cool water down from the bottom of the storage tank into the collector. This process continues as long as the water in the storage tank is cooler than the water in the collector. At night the water in the collector is cooler and heavier so it stays in the collector.

When the hot water in the house is turned on, hot water from the storage tank flows into the cold water inlet of the hot water heater, reducing or eliminating the need for electricity or fuel to heat the water. Cold water from the house supply line then flows into the storage tank and from there to the collector.

There are two major tradeoffs for this simplicity. The first is that the system has to be closed off and drained in the winter, unless it's installed in a part of the country where freezing temperatures are rare. The second is that the storage tank has to be at least a foot above the level of the top of the solar collector or the thermosyphon effect won't work. Heated water won't flow downhill and cold water won't flow uphill unless you install a thermostatically controlled water pump between the storage tank and the solar collector.

In warm parts of the world, the storage tank and collector can be set on the roof, as long as the tank is higher. In northern climates it's safer to put the tank inside the house as we did.

Since the thermosyphon collector heats pressurized water from the house water system, the storage tank has to be both insulated and constructed to hold pressurized hot water. Storage tanks with all the necessary inlets and outlets are available through plumbing supply stores and internet suppliers, but the least expensive way to make one is to adapt a new or slightly used electric tank, which already has the inlets and outlets along with a pressure relief valve (always necessary in any pressurized hot water heating system, even a solar-heated one). However, even if you live in the south, this type of tank must be kept inside the house because it doesn't have a weatherproof exterior.

Thermosyphon tanks must be above the level of the collector in order for the movement of water by thermosyphoning to occur.

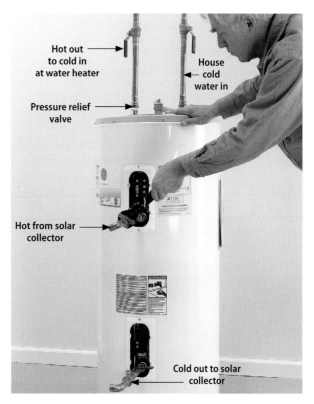

Turn off and disconnect any wiring to the heater you'll be converting to a storage tank. Remove the covers over the heating elements, cut away the wiring, then turn out both heating elements with a socket wrench or a channel lock wrench.

Solder several inches of ¾" pipe to 1" × ¾" reducers so you don't have to use the torch near the plastic and insulation in the water heater. After the pipes cool, wrap the fittings with teflon tape, then thread them into the water heater. Tighten with a wrench, then connect to the PEX lines coming from the solar collector. Connect the house cold water supply to the cold inlet at the top, then connect the hot output to the cold inlet at the main hot water heater.

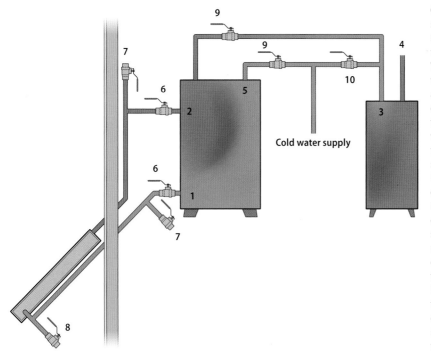

Cool water flows from the bottom of the storage tank (1) to the solar collector, is heated and becomes lighter, then flows to the upper part of the storage tank (2). Water continues to flow until the water in the storage tank is the same temperature as, or warmer than, the water in the solar collector. When hot water is needed, water from the storage tank flows into the cold water inlet of the water heater (3), then to the fixture (4). Cold water from the main supply then flows into the storage tank to be heated (5). In winter, water to the solar collector is shut off (6), and the system is drained (7 and 8). During the winter cold water continues to flow through the storage tank, where it slowly warms to room temperature, reducing the amount of energy needed to heat it. The storage tank can be closed off from the system (9) if necessary, and water can flow directly to the water heater (10). When the solar collector and tank are being filled, the vent/shutoff at the top of the hot water line from the collecter can be opened to vent air.

Storage Tank for a Drainback System

You can save money on a solar hot water system by making your own storage tank from wood, insulation, and an EPDM rubber liner.

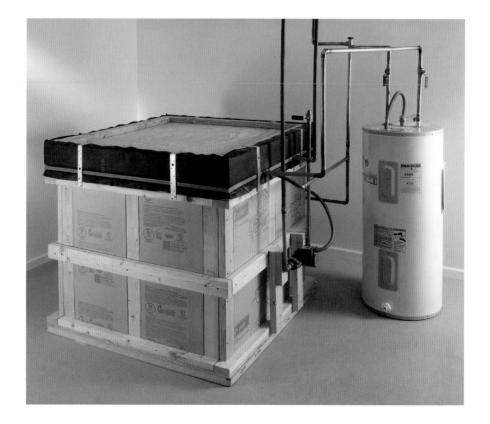

When the sun warms the solar collector, thermostatic controls turn the pump on and cold water is pumped from the storage tank up to the collector. Hot water flows out the top of the collector and down into the storage tank, where the heat is absorbed by water flowing through the heat exchanger coil. Cool water from the bottom of the storage tank is then pumped back to the collector. The storage tank is only partly full and not pressurized, so when the pump turns off, the water in the collector simply drains back into the storage tank, which protects it from freezing.

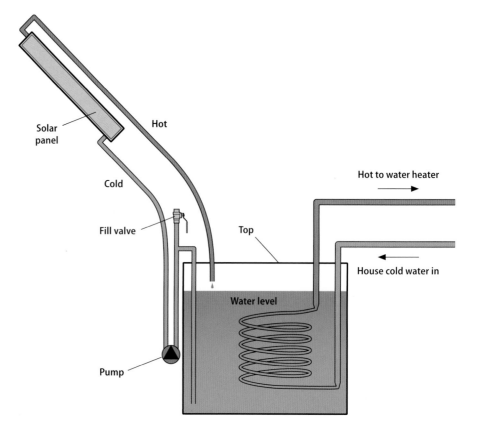

Solar panel

Hot

Cold

Fill valve

Pump

Hot to water heater

Top

House cold water in

Water level

Drainback systems are a tried-and-true option for creating your own hot water from solar heat without worrying about the water freezing on cold nights. The same type of solar collector is used as in a thermosyphon system, but the storage tank can be anywhere inside the house, and the water flow is controlled by a pump. The water in the collector is not pressurized or tied into the potable water system. Heat passes to the pressurized house water system through a heat exchanger—in this case a coil of PEX tubing inside a large storage tank. A temperature sensor on the solar collector turns the pump on when the temperature in the collector is hotter than the temperature in the storage tank, and also turns it off if the water is getting too hot. When the pump is off the water drains back into a storage tank (or separate reservoir in some systems) inside the house. Although power is needed to run the pump and the setup is a little more complicated and expensive than the thermosyphon system, drainback systems are safer and provide more energy savings in cooler climates because they can be used year-round. They are basically automatic, and other than occasionally checking for leaks and general system health, you can safely ignore them most of the time, just like a conventional water heater. A drainback system can also be made large enough to help heat pools and hot tubs, or used as part of a home heating system. An ambitious DIYer with an understanding of plumbing and electricity can build a drainback system, but the plumbing is more complicated, so check the links in the Resources on page 186 for more technical information before you get started. For this project, we are going to focus on building the storage tank.

Storage tanks with built-in heat exchangers are available through plumbing suppliers or the internet, but even a small 40-gallon tank can cost $1,000 or more.

If you have space in a utility area that's well-ventilated and has a drain and a solid, flat, waterproof floor (such as a concrete floor in a basement or insulated garage), you can build your own holding tank from standard building materials. The total cost is a few hundred dollars and you can do it in a day or two. This type of storage tank works well with a drainback system, because it functions as both the reservoir for water from the collectors and as the heat exchanger. A large storage tank storing water from several solar collectors can also be used to provide heat for a hot water heating system. This type of storage tank can't be used for pressurized water, though; the pressurized water is contained in the heat exchanger pipes that run through the storage tank.

The minimum size of the storage tank must be large enough for the heat exchanger piping that you use. For example, one common design uses a 300-foot coil of 1-inch PEX tubing for the heat exchanger, and a coil that size needs roughly 36" × 36" × 30" of space. The bigger the heat exchanger coil, the better, since it's also functioning as storage for the solar-heated hot water that comes out of the house faucets. The maximum size and overall shape depends on the space you have available and on the size of your collectors. For a 4 × 8-foot solar collector, a 36 × 36 × 30 inches storage tank is more than adequate; it takes longer to heat up than a 40-gallon tank, but that means it will retain the heat longer. Generally, a larger tank is better—it doesn't cost much more to build, and you can always add another collector or reduce the amount of water in the tank.

Use rigid insulation on the inside of the tank, both to cushion the EPDM rubber liner and to eliminate heat loss through the wood. Use polyisocyanurate insulation for at least the first layer of insulation under the EPDM; it has a higher R-value, but it also holds up to high heat better than other types of rigid insulation.

TOOLS & MATERIALS

For tank size–3 × 3 × 3' inside	¾" × 4 × 8' sheets plywood	300' roll of 1" PEX tubing
Circular saw	5/4 × 6 × 8 plastic composite deckboards	¾" PEX (as needed)
Miter saw	1" × 4 × 8' sheets rigid	¾" PEX elbows
Drill/driver with bits	polyisocyanurate insulation	¾" PEX T
Caulk gun	12 × 16' 45-mil EPDM liner	¾" shutoff (for PEX)
Razor knife	2" × 4 × 8' XPS polystyrene insulation	(2) 1 × ¾" PEX coupling
4' level	1½" × 4 × 8' XPS polystyrene insulation	Thermostatic controller for pump
Scissors	Deck screws (1⅝", 2½")	Inline or submersible pump
Stapler	Construction adhesive compatible	(for drainback system)
Clamps	with foamboard	(2) Strips weatherseal
2 × 4" × 8'	Stainless-steel staples	Eye and ear protection
½" × 4 × 8' sheets plywood	Silicone caulk	Work gloves

CUTTING LIST

KEY	NUMBER	DIMENSION	PART	MATERIAL
A	8	1½" × 3½" × 41"	Frame	SPF
B	12	1½" × 3½" × 33½"	Studs	SPF
C	8	1½" × 3½" × 48"	Frame	SPF
D	2	1½" × 3½" × 47"	Frame	SPF
E	2	1½" × 3½" × 44"	Frame	SPF
F	2	¾" × 48" × 48"	Base, top	Plywood
G	2	½" × 41" × 38"	Sides	Plywood
H	2	½" × 40" × 38"	Sides	Plywood
I	2	1" × 5½" × 37"	Rail	Composite decking
J	2	1" × 5½" × 48"	Rail	Composite decking
K	2	2" × 48" × 48"	Insulation	Polystyrene
L	2	1" × 40" × 40"	Insulation	Polyisocyanurate
M	1	1" × 48" × 48"	Top insulation	Polyisocyanurate
N	2	1" × 40" × 36"	Insulation	Polyisocyanurate
O	4	1" × 38" × 36"	Insulation	Polyisocyanurate
P	2	1" × 36" × 36"	Insulation	Polyisocyanurate
Q	4	1½" × 33½" × 15¼"	Outer insulation	Polystyrene
R	4	1½" × 33½" × 16¾"	Outer insulation	Polystyrene

STORAGE TANK

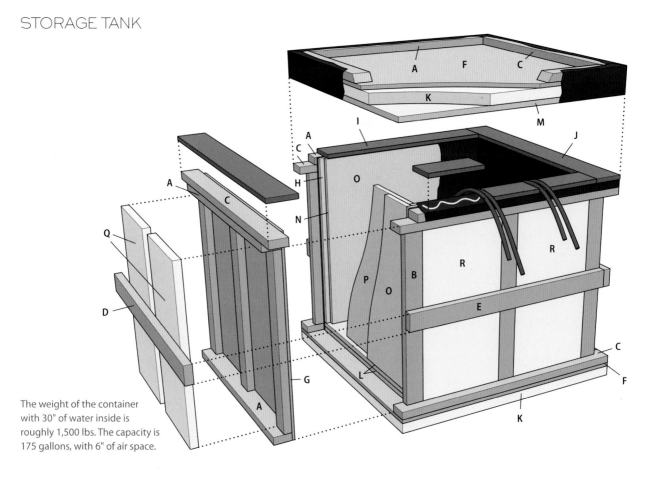

The weight of the container with 30" of water inside is roughly 1,500 lbs. The capacity is 175 gallons, with 6" of air space.

How to Build the Tank

Select a flat, level area of floor for the storage tank, preferably not too far away from the plumbing for your solar collector and water heater. When the tank is full of water it will weigh roughly 1,500 lbs., so it needs to sit on a solid, flat base. If the floor is uneven, level it with floor leveler or build a wood platform. Although the

tank will be sealed shut with no penetrations through the liner, with this much water it's best to be prudent and place the tank in the vicinity of a floor drain or an area where water won't cause any damage. And be sure to keep the tank bolted shut, especially if you have kids—the water inside can get dangerously hot.

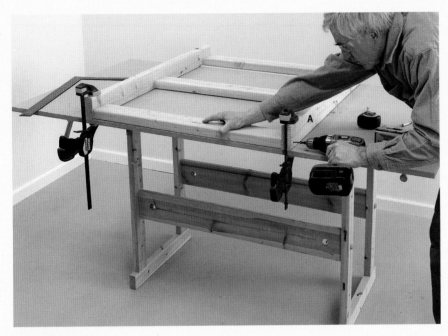

1 Screw two of the 41" 2 × 4s to three vertical 2 × 4s, then fasten the 41"-wide piece of ½" plywood to the 2 × 4s with construction adhesive and 1⅝" screws. Repeat for the opposite side. Align the bottom edge of the plywood with the bottom 2 × 4; the top edge will overhang 1½".

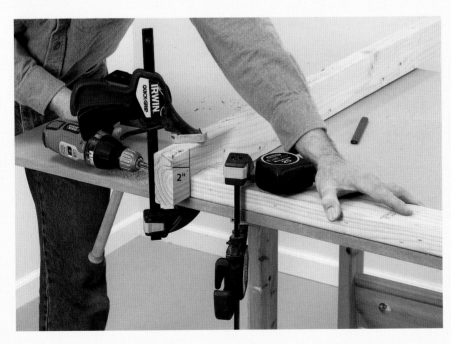

2 Assemble the remaining sides, but instead of aligning the horizontal studs with the edge, fasten them 2" in from the edges. Place the third stud in the center.

continued on page 134

3 Place the ¾" plywood base at the tank location, then connect the short sides to the long sides, fastening the overlapping corner 2 × 4s together with the long deck screws.

4 Turn the box on its side. Fasten the plywood sides in place on the long walls, taking care to align corners and edges. Check the box for square as you assemble it.

5 Tip the box over, then glue and screw the plywood base to the 2 × 4 frame, aligning all the edges.

6 Glue the 2" foam base to the plywood base with construction adhesive, then turn the box right-side up and add the second layer of 2 × 4s to the top, overlapping the corners for strength. Screw the plywood walls to the final layer of 2 × 4s.

7 Place the polyiso insulation inside the box, using the foamboard adhesive to attach it. You don't need much; the water will hold the insulation in place. Add the second layer, then seal all the corners on the bottom and sides with silicone caulk.

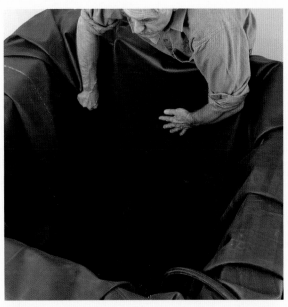

8 Cut and set aside a 5 × 12' piece of the EPDM for the top, then fold the remainder into the tank. Work it into the corners, leaving the rubber loose at the bottom so it doesn't stretch with the weight of the water. Add 6" of water to hold the rubber in place as you fold over the corners. Drape the excess over the sides.

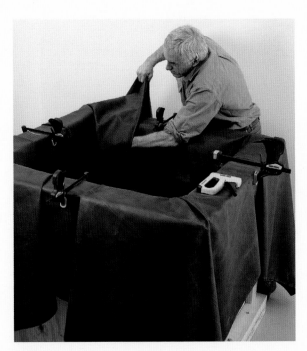

9 Fold the corners as neatly as possible and clamp them in place. Don't stretch the rubber—leave it sagging at the bottom.

10 Staple the rubber around the outside edge of the top 2 × 4 ledge.

continued on page 136

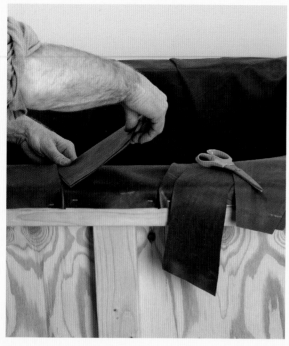

11 Level out the rubber ledge between the corner folds with scrap pieces of rubber.

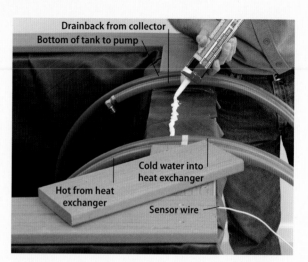

Drainback from collector
Bottom of tank to pump
Cold water into heat exchanger
Hot from heat exchanger
Sensor wire

12 Decide on a plumbing layout and strap stubs of ¾" PEX to the top edge for the plumbing connections. Purchase a thermostatic controller for the pump that will circulate water between the tank and the solar collector, and run one of the sensor wires into the tank. Cut the pieces of 5/4 × 6 cap, then set them on a bead of silicone and screw them in place with 2½" deck or stainless steel screws. *NOTE: If you use copper instead of PEX, complete all soldered connections into and out of the tank before placing the copper to avoid melting the EPDM liner.*

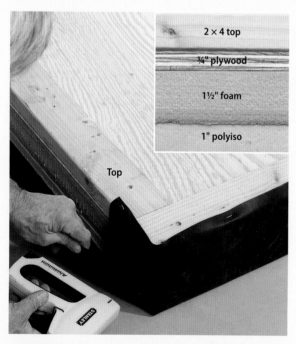

2 × 4 top
¾" plywood
1½" foam
1" polyiso
Top

13 Construct the top from 2 × 4s, ¾" plywood, 1½ or 2" rigid foam, and 1" polyiso. Cut a 5' square of rubber liner for the top, with 6" cutouts at each corner. Fold the flaps up the sides and over the top, then staple the rubber in place.

14 Place 1½" pieces of insulation on the sides, then install horizontal 2 × 4s around the center. If desired, you can add pieces of insulation above and below the 2 × 4s, then cover the sides with ¼" plywood for a finished appearance.

15 Set the 1" PEX tubing into the tank, then connect the ends to the incoming and outgoing ¾" tubing with PEX 1 × ¾" reducers. Leave enough slack in the PEX lines so that they can move around as they fill. After making the connections, temporarily hook one end (outside the tank) to the water hose and plug the other end, then turn the water on and check for leaks in your connections. Then fill the tubing with water. *TIP: Wrap a concrete block in EPDM and set it in the bottom to keep the PEX tubing above the cooler water at the bottom.*

16 Add two strips of weatherseal on the ledge about 2" apart. Use a soft foam type that compresses easily and fills voids, like this (inset).

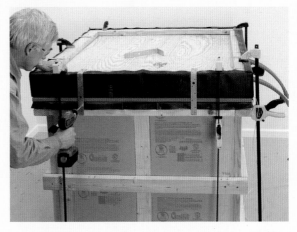

17 Complete the plumbing connections inside the tank, fill gaps around the pipes on the ledge with silicone, then clamp the top down tightly to seal the edges. Fasten the top to the base with galvanized straps and deck screws.

Adding Water

The water used in the collecter tank is pumped to the solar collector, heated, and then drained back to the tank, dripping into the air space. It is at atmospheric pressure and is not connected to the house water system. If possible, use distilled water for the tank to avoid mineral deposits. If that's too expensive, house water will work. If all the openings are well-sealed and there are no leaks, the tank will stay full. Drain the old water and replace it every year or two.

Add the water to about six inches from the top after making all the plumbing connections and filling the PEX tubing. Test the system before sealing the top to make sure everything works.

Check the water level from time to time, especially in the first months. You can either just open the top, or else drill a hole for a ½" pipe in the top, seal around it, put a threaded cap on, and then check the water level with a dipstick.

continued on page 138

Installing a Tempering Valve

Solar hot water can get dangerously hot on sunny summer days—up to 180° F, much hotter than the 120° water in a typical hot water heater. To avoid scalding when using solar hot water, add a tempering (or mixing) valve above the hot water outlet on the hot water heater—a valve that automatically lowers the temperature of hot water when necessary by mixing in cold. Installation is straightforward. Turn off the hot and cold water and drain the system, then cut the supply pipes as necessary and install the valve.

Most external pumps are water-lubricated, and since water seeks its own level the pump should be attached near the bottom of the tank. Connect the pump to the cold-water side of the system, to a pipe run to the bottom of the tank, and prime it with water before turning the system on for the first time. Different solar collector systems need different size pumps: consult the dealer or a professional installer for help selecting the right size. Wire the pump to a power source and to a "differential controller"—a type of thermostatic control that switches on when the collector is warmer than the storage tank, following the instructions for the control. Connect the water lines to the collector and to the potable water lines as shown in the photo. *NOTE: Use pipe straps and blocking as necessary to secure the pipes. We've omitted them from this photo for clarity.*

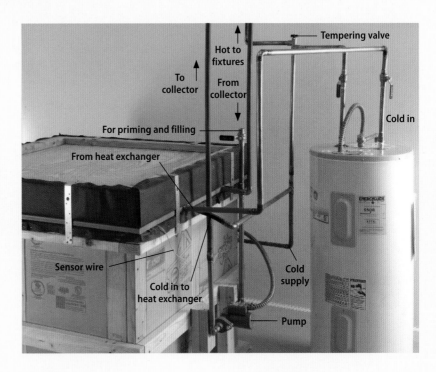

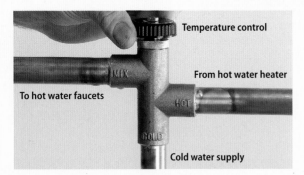

Install the tempering valve on the hot water line after it comes out of the heater, before it goes to any fixtures. Connect it to the cold water line. Then reconnect the hot water supply for the house fixtures to the outlet marked "Mix." If you buy a valve with sweat connections, remove the knob and the thermostatic controls inside the valve before soldering, then reinstall them when the pipes are cool.

They are not required, but you may also wish to install a few thermometers in your system: one for measuring the temperature of water coming from the collector, and one for checking the temperature of water coming from the tempering valve. Thermometers with threaded fittings are available at plumbing-supply stores and online. *NOTE: Design inspired by Gary Reysa at builditsolar.com*

Other Types of Solar Collectors

Pressurized, closed-loop system: This system uses propylene glycol mixed with water, and is commonly used in cold climates. The heat is transferred to a storage tank by way of a heat exchanger, and a pump and controller are used to move the antifreeze through the system. In order for the system to be absolutely safe (and to meet code requirements) the heat exchanger pipes must be double-walled, so that if a leak does develop it won't contaminate the potable water. The antifreeze also must be propylene glycol, a less toxic type of antifreeze. Don't use ethylene glycol (the type used in cars).

This type of system requires an expansion tank and other special components, and should be installed only by an expert or by a highly qualified DIYer. Plans and finished work must be approved by a plumbing inspector.

Evacuated-tube collector: This type of collector has to be purchased from a supplier, although homeowners can install it. Water pipes in this system, instead of running through an insulated box, are installed inside a round tube of insulated glass. The vacuum inside the insulated glass allows light through, but slows heat loss. Evacuated-tube collectors are more efficient than flat-plate collectors in partially sunny or cloudy conditions.

Batch heaters: Instead of pipes, the storage tank itself is mounted outside in a large, insulated heat collector box. It can be mounted above or below the water heater, because pressurized house water flows through it whenever hot water is called for. Batch heaters are sold commercially and can also be made from scratch by a resourceful homeowner, but like the thermosyphon system are generally not suitable for cold climates because of the risk of freezing pipes.

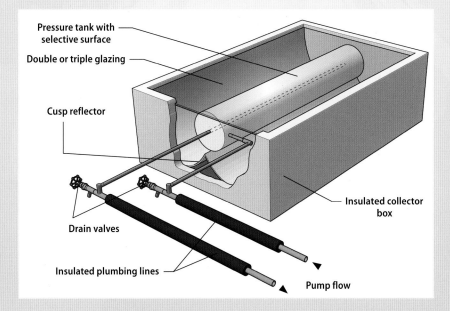

Pressure tank with selective surface

Double or triple glazing

Cusp reflector

Drain valves

Insulated plumbing lines

Insulated collector box

Pump flow

Solar Hot Air Collector— Window Mount

One of the simplest and most cost-effective ways to harvest solar power is with a hot air collector. If you stand in front of a south-facing window on a sunny day, even in winter, you'll understand the basic idea. A solar hot air collector absorbs heat from the sun on a black metal plate in a large, insulated box, then the heat is transferred to cool air flowing over the metal plate from inside the house. As the warmer, lighter air rises out the top of the collector into the house, cooler air from the lower part of the house is drawn in at the bottom of the collector.

Large hot air collectors built into walls are capable of heating a whole house on sunny days. This window collector won't do that unless you live in a super-insulated house, but it can still make a dent in your heating bills. And it's designed to be removable, so in the warm months when you don't need it you can just take out a few screws and store it in the garage, then put the window air conditioner in.

There is no standard size for this collector; make it as wide as your window and 4 to 6 feet long. The lower end can either be set against the ground, if it's close enough, or attached to the house with wood braces. Place it in a south-facing window that gets at least five or six hours of direct sun every day, and don't forget to close the flaps when the sun goes down so you don't lose all the heat you gained.

SOLAR HOT AIR COLLECTOR

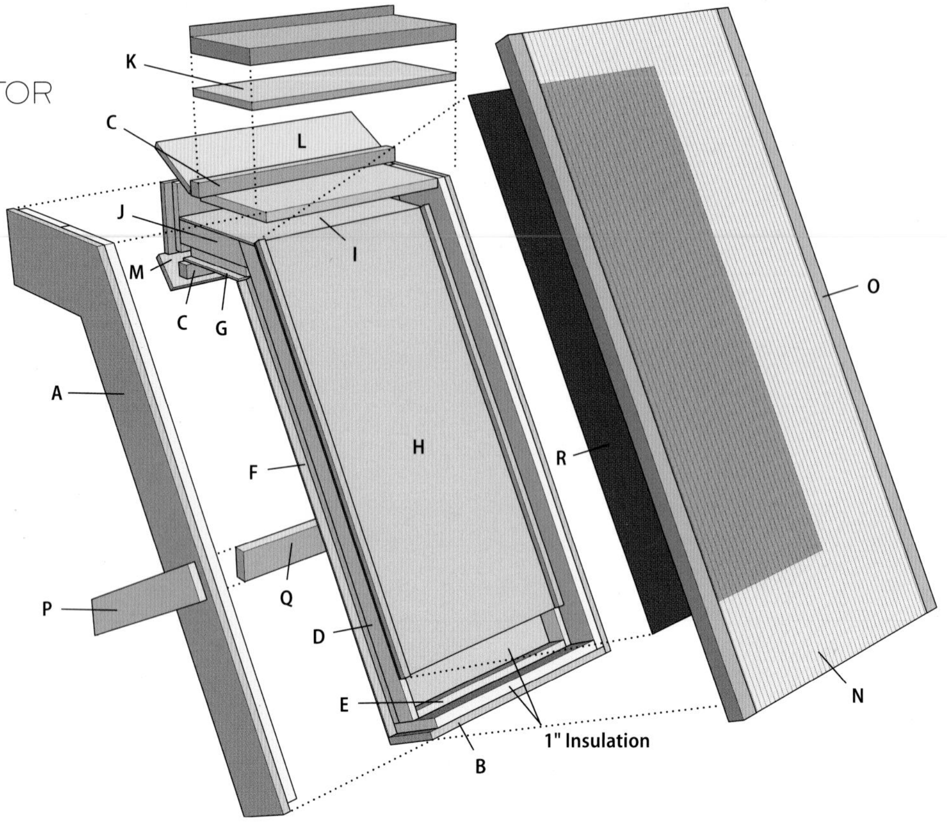

TOOLS & MATERIALS

Circular saw
Miter saw
Jigsaw
Drill/driver with bits
Triangle square
Angle measure
4-ft. level
Caulk gun
Razor knife
Tin snips
Clamps
Tape measure
¼" × 4 × 8 plywood
¾" × 4 × 8 AC or BC grade (one paint-grade side) exterior plywood
1 × 3" × 8' cedar or treated (for outside supports)
2 × 2" × width of window pine or hardwood
1" × 8 × 8' (rip to size for doors)
1" × 4 × 8' polyisocyanurate insulation
Foam backer rod
Hinges
Self-adhesive weatherseal
Doublewall polycarbonate with tape or caps for ends (available from glass stores, greenhouse suppliers, or online)
Black aluminum sheet or 16" wide brown aluminum coil stock
Black high-heat paint
1½ × 96 × 1/16"-thick aluminum angle
1¼" deck screws
1⅝" deck screws
2¼" drywall screws
1½" neoprene screws
1" metal angle brackets
½" × 6 sheet-metal screws or stainless-steel staples
Construction adhesive (look for quick-gripping type compatible with foam insulation)
Clear silicone caulk
Aluminum tape
Eye and ear protection
Work gloves

CUTTING LIST

KEY	NUMBER	DIMENSION	PART	MATERIAL
A	2	¾" × 64" × 19"	Sides	Plywood
B	2	¾" × 24 7/16" × 7½"	Ends	Plywood
C	2	1½" × 1½" × 25⅞"	Stops	2 × 2
D	2	¾" × 2½" × 48"	Side nailers	1 × 3
E	1	¾" × 2½" × 20¾"	End nailer	1 × 3
F	1	¼" × 46" × 24½"	Back	Plywood
G	1	¼" × 10" × 24½"	Upper back	Plywood
H	1	¼" × 44" × 22½"	Divider	Plywood
I	1	¼" × 14¼" × 22½"	Upper divider	Plywood
J	2	¾" × 2½" × 14"	Upper nailer	1 × 3
K	1	¾" × 10¼" × 25⅞"	Top cap	Plywood
L	1	¾" × 7¼" × 25⅞"	Top door	1 × 8
M	1	¾" × 4" × 25⅞"	Bottom door	1 × 6
N	1	52" × 25⅞"	Glazing	Polycarbonate
O	2	1½" × 1½" × 53"	Corners	Aluminum
P	2	¾" × 3½" × 25½"	Side brace	1 × 4 PT
Q	1	1½" × 3½" × 25⅞"	Back brace	2 × 4 PT
R	1	44" × 22½"	Heat absorber	Aluminum

NOTE: All dimensions are for a 26" wide window opening 4' off the ground. Adjust for your window.

☀ How to Build the Collector

1 Mark a piece of plywood at the angle recommended for your latitude (see page 125). This collector will face the sun at a 60° angle, but to make the best use of the plywood we're cutting the short horizontal side, so the triangle square is set at 30°. The length of the collector is 4' (measured on the bottom), based on the available space from the window to the ground. The short side is initially cut long, because the easiest way to cut it to exact length is to mark it in place. Make the two sides mirror images, with the best side of the plywood facing out.

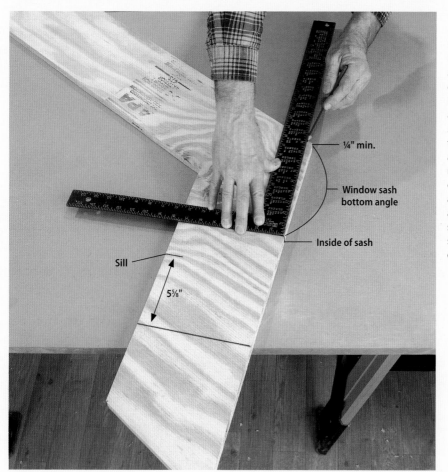

2 Set one of the pieces in the window opening, with the short side level and sitting on the inside sill and the outside tight against the outside sill. Mark the edge of the inside sill and the inside of the window sash. Mark and cut the end of the short piece 5⅝" from the window sill mark at the bottom. To create a slope and a tight fit with the sash on the top, measure the angle of the bottom of the window sash with an angle measure, then transfer that angle to the top of the plywood, starting at the inside edge of the sash. Trim this top edge with a circular saw.

continued on page 144

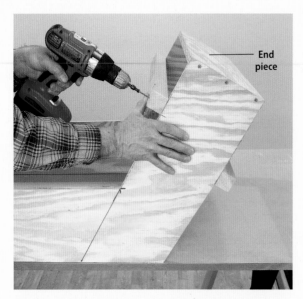

End piece

3 Measure the distance between the stop moldings holding the window sash in, then subtract 1½" to get the length of the end pieces, which fit inside the side pieces. Predrill and screw the end pieces in place, then fasten 2 × 2s across the frame at the sash and sill locations.

4 Line the sides and ends with 1" polyisocyanurate insulation. Leave the foil side facing into the box and glue the insulation in place with construction adhesive. Wrap the exposed upper edges with aluminum foil tape to protect the insulation from UV rays. Cut the insulation ¼" narrower than the plywood sides so that the bottom piece of ¼" plywood will fit in between the sides.

5 Screw the 1 × 3 nailers to the sides of both the long and short pieces using 2¼" screws. Place the nailers 1¼" from the bottom edge to leave room for 1" insulation and ¼" plywood.

6 Fasten ¼" plywood to the top of the 1 × 3 to divide the incoming cool air from the hot air. Leave a 3" gap at the lower end of the plywood for air flow. Butt the two pieces of plywood together at the bend, then cover the small gap with a double layer of aluminum tape. Caulk the gaps at the end and at the corners of the insulation.

7 Turn the box over, add the 1" insulation to the bottom of the box, then cover it with the ¼" plywood. Glue the plywood to the insulation and screw it to the 1 × 3 nailer with 2¼" screws.

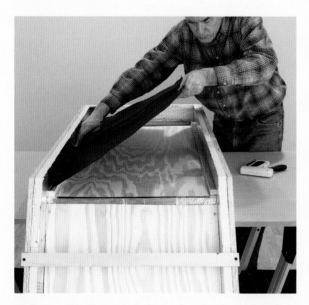

8 Cut two ¾" nailers an inch shorter than the plywood divider, then fasten them to the plywood and the 1 × 3 to create an air channel above and below the heat-absorbing aluminum. Cut the aluminum to fit across the box, then attach it to the nailers with stainless-steel staples or ½" sheet-metal screws. *NOTE: We used a thick, pre-painted aluminum sheet that's available online. If you use aluminum coil stock, paint it black after installing it. See Resources on page 186.*

9 Cut and install 1" polyiso insulation to fit the angled top, from the 2 × 2 to the outside corner. Caulk any gaps along the sides. Spread a bead of glue on the insulation, then cover it with ¾" plywood screwed across the top, and extending from the 2 × 2 to 1" beyond the outside corner. Clamp the plywood and insulation until the glue sets.

continued on page 146

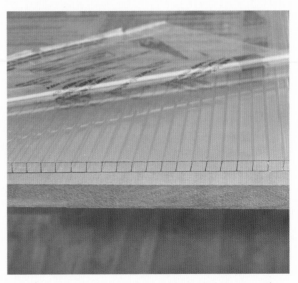

10 Cut the polycarbonate glazing so that it matches the width of the box. Cut it long enough so it tucks under the overhang at the top and hangs over ½" at the bottom. Make sure to install it with the UV-protected side up (the side with the label).

11 The vertical ribs add strength and insulation value to lightweight doublewall polycarbonate, and the two layers help it resist fogging. Cover the top end with waterproof tape and the bottom end with a permeable tape that keeps bugs out.

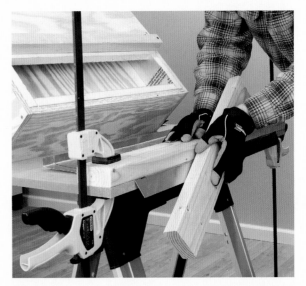

12 Spread silicone on the plywood edge and set the glazing in place, pushing it under the plywood edge at the top and clamping the bottom to hold it in place. Predrill holes in the aluminum corner before you set it in place, and cut the upper end to fit the angle of the top. Spread a bead of silicone about 1" from the outside edge of the glazing and set the aluminum corner over it. Hold the aluminum down firmly and evenly and screw it to the plywood sides with the 1½" screws. Clamp the glazing at the bottom for a few hours until the silicone sets up.

13 Cut aluminum or galvanized coil stock to cover the top, measuring from the 2 × 2. Cut it 3" longer and wider, then clamp the coil stock between the table and a piece of wood and make a 1½" bend at the front and the rear. The front and rear bends should go in opposite directions. Make a 1½" cut on both sides 1½" in from the front and back so that the sides can bend down. Place the coil stock on the top of the plywood, with the back bent up tight against the 2 × 2 so it fits behind the window. Then fold the front down over the glazing and bend the excess back around the sides. Finally, fold the sides down and screw them in place with the ½" screws.

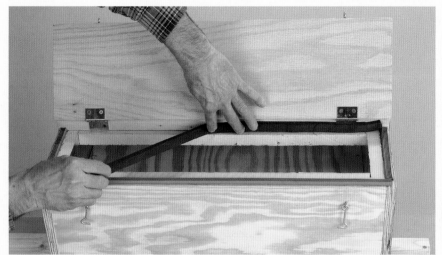

14 Cut 1 × 8s to fit for covers for the inlet and outlet, so that heat won't be lost when the sun goes down. Apply self-adhesive weatherseal around the edges, then screw on two or three hinges, depending on the width of the window. Use hooks to hold the upper cover in place and small barrel bolts to hold the lower cover.

15 Set the solar collector in the window with the inside 2 × 2 tight against the sash and the outside pushed against the sill (you'll need a helper for this). Fasten 1 × 3 supports to the sides, then screw them to the house with metal angle brackets or a 2 × 4 between the supports. Attach the collector to the window sash on the inside with small angle brackets placed on the 2 × 2. Wedge foam backer rod or other type of weatherseal into gaps around the window jamb and into the gap between the upper and lower sash.

Working with Doublewall Polycarbonate

Doublewall polycarbonate is often used in greenhouses—and for solar projects—because it's lightweight, has some insulation value, and doesn't fog over with condensation. It's also much less expensive, much lighter, and much less breakable than insulated glass. It can be cut easily with a saw, and it transmits almost as much light as insulated glass. Most suppliers carry it in 4' and 6' widths and up to 20' in length (look for greenhouse or plastics suppliers in your area, or check online).

One side of the polycarbonate has UV protection that keeps it from getting hazy and cracked, as happens with standard plexiglas. Make sure you install the panels with this side facing up. Once installed, the top of a panel is sealed with waterproof foil tape or caps; the bottom is sealed with a breathable tape that keeps dust and bugs out but lets moisture drain through.

Polycarbonate is cut and drilled with standard woodworking tools. Use a blade with 10 to 12 teeth per inch, such as a fine-toothed plywood cutting blade. Polycarbonate moves with temperature changes, so drill holes 1/16" larger than the fasteners and don't overtighten. The panels are fastened with neoprene screws (screws with wide heads and neoprene rubber washers attached). A wide variety of glazing accessories for joints, corners, and roof caps is available if you make a larger project.

Solar Hot Air Collector—Roof Mount

The solar hotbox works on the same general principle as the window hot air collector in the previous project, but it's a big step up in size and amount of heat generated. Designed to work with an existing forced-air heating system, this hotbox can carry a substantial amount of the heating load for an average residence—up to 40 percent for the home where this project was done. With gas prices rising all the time, that can quickly add up to serious money.

As always, the most cost-effective way to save money on energy costs is by sealing air leaks and adding more insulation, but once you've done that, this project is a good next step. Mounted on a south-facing wall or on the roof, the collector takes air from inside your home and blows it through the thermal solar panels, which are essentially a series of metal ducts in a black box under tempered glass. As the air moves through the ductwork, the sun's rays cause it to heat to high temperatures. Then, at the end of the duct, another vent moves the air back into your home's heating ductwork or an interior vent, sending the now-heated air right into the home. It's basically a forced-air heater that uses the sun for heat instead of gas burners.

The flow of air is controlled by a fan and vent dampers. The fan only turns on when the thermostat calls for heat and the temperature in the hotbox is higher than the temperature in the house, so there's no heat loss during the night or on cloudy days, even though the hotbox requires two holes cut in the roof. It's also possible to put a variation of this design on a south-facing wall, as long as it gets at least six hours of sunlight per day.

When combined, these three DIY "hotboxes" introduce enough hot air into this home to carry 30 to 40% of the home heating load.

You can build solar hot air panels yourself. The style shown here is simple: essentially, a box, a series of ducts, and a piece of glass. The panels are permanently installed and ducted in to your home, complete with automated thermostatic controls. In this project, we'll walk you through one version of a solar hot air panel designed and installed by Applied Energy Innovations of Minneapolis, Minnesota (see Resources page 186), with the help of homeowner Scott Travis.

Anatomy of a Hot Air Solar Panel

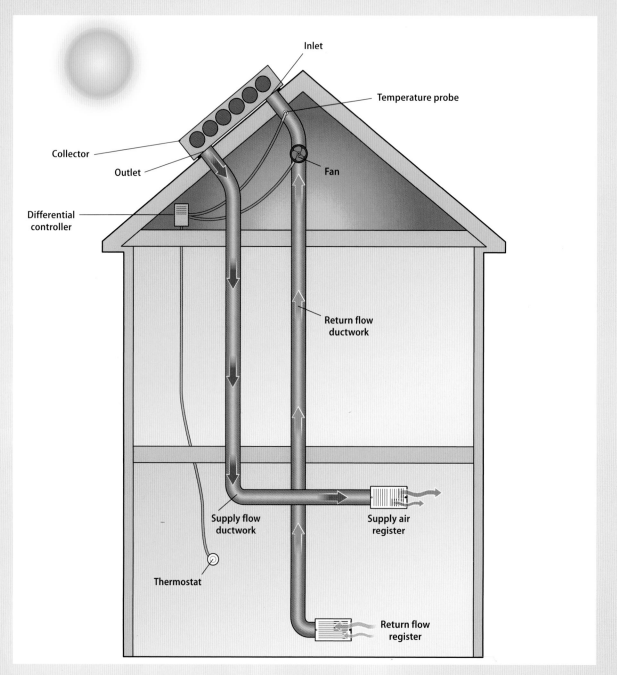

The solar hot box is a very simple system. Cold air from the house is drawn up into a network of ducts in the collector, where it is warmed by the sun then circulated inside to heat the house.

TOOLS & MATERIALS

Metal-cutting saw
Drywall saw
Straightedge
Aviation snips
Tape measure
Temperature controls
Eye and ear protection
Carpenter's square
Drill/driver with bits
⅛" pop rivets
Pop rivet gun
Caulk gun

Aluminum foil tape
Rubber gasket roofing nails
2 × 6 steel studs
Utility knife
8" blower fan
4" hole saw
Trim paint roller
Sheet-metal screws
  with rubber gaskets
Chalkline
Scissors
Reciprocating saw

Roof jack
High-temperature
  black paint (matte)
4" aluminum HVAC duct
1"-wide closed-cell foam gasket
4" male and female
  duct connectors
(2) 8" plenum box
High-temperature silicone caulk
Cardboard
Sheet-metal start collars
Roofing cement

1"-thick R7 rigid insulation
¼" tempered glass
Flashing
Shingles (if needed)
Unistrut
Unistrut connectors
(2) Duct collars
⅜" threaded rod
Spring-fed 8"
  backdraft dampers
Work gloves

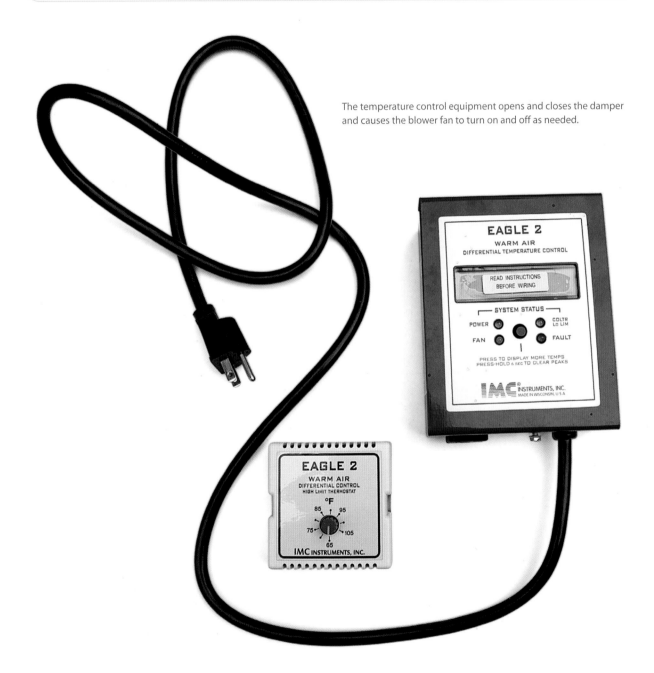

The temperature control equipment opens and closes the damper and causes the blower fan to turn on and off as needed.

How to Build a Solar Hot Air Panel

1 Cut and bend the box frame pieces from 2 × 6 steel studs. Each steel stud piece will wrap two sides of the panel with a 90° corner bend. Mark the bend location on both steel studs. Cut a relief into the 6" side of the stud with aviation snips at this mark. Bend the stud to an L-shape and use a square to ensure that the corner forms a true 90° angle.

2 Drill ⅛"-dia. holes in the overlapping top and bottom flanges. Clamp the corners together before drilling, using a square to make sure the corner forms a 90° angle.

3 Fasten the corners of the metal box with two ⅛"-dia. sheet-metal pop rivets in the top and bottom. Leave one corner open to create access for the insulation panel insert.

4 Cut the foil-faced rigid foam insulation to match the interior dimensions of the box, using a drywall saw or a utility knife.

5 Apply high-temperature silicone to the bottom flanges of the box (inset). Fit the 1" foil-faced insulation from step #4 into the back of the frame, then close up the box and secure the open corner. Cut 5"-wide strips of foam insulation to the length and width of the panel. Place a thick bead of silicone around the outside perimeter of the unit. Insert the strips into the silicone and press tightly against the sides of the panel to hold the backing firmly in place. The foil should be facing into the box.

6 Seal the insulation edges. Place a bead of silicone around the inside corner where the insulation strips and backing panel meet, and then seal with foil tape. Flip the panel over. Place a bead of silicone on the intersection of the 2 × 6 stud flange and the back of the insulation, and seal with foil tape. Conceal any exposed insulation edges with foil tape.

7 Create inlet and outlet holes in the walls with a hole saw or circle cutter. The number and location of the ductwork holes depends on where each panel fits into the overall array (presuming you are making and installing multiple panels). The first and last panels in the series will each have one end wall that is uncut, while intermediate panels will have duct holes on each end wall (inset).

8 Install a compartment separator in the first and last panels with a piece of foil insulation set on edge. Cut ductwork access holes in the separator. Then, cut out holes for the ductwork that will pass through the separator. Also cut a plenum opening in the separated compartment in the first and last unit.

continued on page 154

9 Paint the entire box interior using black high-temperature paint and allow it to dry completely. A trim roller works well for this task.

10 Insert the ductwork. Beginning at the inlet duct, guide 4" aluminum HVAC ductwork in a serpentine shape throughout the entire multi-panel installation, ending at the outlet duct. Join ends of adjoining duct sections with flexible duct connectors fashioned into a U shape and secured with metal screws and foil tape. Paint each section of ductwork with black high-temperature paint once it is in place.

11 Paint the last section of ductwork and touch up around the interior of the box so all exposed surfaces are black.

12 Affix the glass top. First, double-check that all openings in the panel are adequately sealed and insulated. Then, line the tops of the steel stud frame with foam closed-cell gasket tape. Carefully position the glass on top of the gasket tape, lined up ½" from the outside of the frame on all sides. Then, position foam closed-cell gasket tape around the perimeter of the top of the glass panel.

13 Attach the casing. Work with a local metal shop to bend metal flashing that will wrap your panel box. Attach it around the perimeter of the panel with sheet-metal screws with rubber washer heads. *TIP: Be careful when working around the plenum ductwork. If you set the unit down on its back side, you will force the plenum up and break the seal around the opening.*

14 Mark off the panel layout locations on the roof. Transfer the locations of the 8"-dia. inlet and outlet holes to the roof as well. The location of these holes should not interfere with the structural framing members of your roof (either rafters or trusses). Adjust the panel layout slightly to accommodate the best locations of the inlet and outlet, according to your roof's setup. Cut out the inlet and outlet holes with a reciprocating saw.

15 Use a roof jack to form an 8"-dia. opening. Apply a heavy double bead of roofing cement along the top and sides of the jack. Nail the perimeter of the flange using rubber gasket nails. Cut and install shingles with roofing cement to fit over the flashing so they lie flat against the flange.

16 Attach Unistrut mounting U-channel bars to the roof for each panel. Use the chalklines on the roof to determine the position of the Unistrut, and attach to the roof trusses with Unistrut connectors.

continued on page 156

17 Hoist the panels into position. Carefully follow safety regulations and use scaffolding, ladders, ropes, and lots of helpers to hoist the panels onto the roof. Wear fall-arresting gear and take care not to allow the plenum ductwork to be damaged.

18 Connect the inlet and outlet ducts on the panel(s) to the openings on the roof. Position the panels so the inlet and outlet openings match perfectly, and attach with a duct collar and silicone caulk.

19 Connect the panels to the Unistrut with a ⅜" threaded rod attached at the top and bottom of the panel on the outside. Cut threaded rod to size, then attach to the Unistrut with Unistrut nuts. Attach the top clip to the top of the rod and the front face of the panel. Tighten the assembly to compress the panel down to the Unistrut for a tight hold.

20 Seal the panel connections with 1" foam gasket tape around each end of the panels where they connect. Place a bead of silicone caulk on top of the gasket tape and then attach 3"-wide flashing over the two panels at the joint. Attach flashing to the panel with galvanized sheet-metal screws with rubber gasket heads.

21 Hook up the interior ductwork, including dampers and a blower fan. The manner in which this is done will vary tremendously depending on your house structure and how you plan to integrate the supplementary heat. You will definitely want to work with a professional HVAC contractor (preferably one with solar experience) for this part of the job.

Another Type of Solar Heater

Manufactured solar air heaters are available in a variety of sizes and styles and can be built in or attached to an existing wall or roof.

A solar air heater was built into the framing of the wall, with the siding trimmed around it (see Resources, page 186).

Solar Still

Make your own distilled water from stream or lake water, salt water, or even brackish, dirty water, using this simple solar distiller. With just a few basic building materials, a sheet of glass, and some sunshine, you can purify your own water at no cost and with minimal effort.

Distilled water is not just for drinking, and it's always worth keeping a few gallons of it on hand. Clean water free of chemicals and minerals has a number of valuable uses:

- Always refill the lead-acid batteries used for solar energy systems or automobiles with distilled water.
- Water delicate plants such as orchids with distilled water; minerals and additives such as fluoride or chlorine that are present in most tap water can harm plants.
- Distilled water mixed with antifreeze is recommended for car radiators, as it's less corrosive.
- Steam irons become clogged with mineral deposits unless you use distilled water.

The principle of using the sun's heat to separate water from dissolved minerals has been understood for millenia, salt ponds being the best example of how this knowledge has been put to use in the past. In salt ponds, seawater is drained into shallow ponds and then baked and purified in the sun until all that remains are crystals of salt. In this case, the pure water that gradually evaporated away was considered a useless byproduct, but as far back as the time of the ancient Greeks it was known that seawater could be made fresh and drinkable by this process.

A solar still works like a salt evaporation pond, except that the water that invisibly evaporates is extracted from the air; the minerals and other impurities are left behind and discarded. As the hot, moisture-laden air rises up to the slanting sheet of relatively cool glass sealed to the box, water condenses out in the form of small droplets that cling to the glass. As these droplets get heavier, they roll down the glass to the collector tube at the bottom and then out to the jug.

Distill your own crystal clear, chemical-free drinking water with a solar distiller.

Solar Still

The box is built from ¾-inch BC-grade plywood, painted black on the inside to absorb heat. We used a double layer of plywood on the sides to resist warping and to help insulate the box, with an insulated door at the back and a sheet of glass on top.

Finding a good lining or container to hold the water in the inside of the box as it heats and evaporates can be complicated. The combination of high heat and water containing salt or other contaminents can corrode metals faster than usual and cause plastic containers to break down or off-gas, imparting an unpleasant taste to the distilled water. The best liners are glass or stainless steel, although you can also coat the inside of the box with two or three coats of black silicone caulk (look for an FDA-listed type approved for use around food). Spread the caulk around the bottom and sides with a taping knife. After it dries and cures thoroughly, just pour water in—the silicone is impervious to the heat and water.

We chose to paint the inside black and use two large glass baking pans to hold the water. Glass baking pans are a safe, inexpensive container for dirty or salty water, and they can easily be removed for cleaning. We used two 10 × 15-inch pans, which hold up to 8 quarts of water when full. To increase the capacity of the still, just increase the size of the wooden box and add more pans.

The operation of the distiller is simple. As the temperature inside the box rises, water in the pans heats up and evaporates, rising up to the angled glass, where it slowly runs down to the collector tube and then out to a container.

The runoff tube is made from 1-inch PEX tubing. Stainless steel can also be used. However, use caution with other materials—if in doubt, boil a piece of the material in tap water for 10 minutes, then taste the water after it cools to see if it added any flavor. If it did, don't use it.

Turn undrinkable water into pure, crystal-clear distilled water with a home-built solar still.

TOOLS & MATERIALS

Drill/driver with bits
Circular saw
Triangle square
Straightedge
Caulk gun
Razor knife
Clamps
Tape measure

2 × 4 × 8' pressure treated wood
(1) ¾ × 4' × 8' sheet of BC exterior plywood
(2) 1½" galvanized hinges
Self-adhesive weatherseal (8')
Knob or drawer pull
27¼ × 22 × ⅛" (minimum) glass
Silicone caulk
High-temperature black paint

1" PEX tubing
(2) 10 × 15" glass baking pans
Wood glue
Deck screws (1¼", 2", 2½")
Painter's tape
Eye and ear protection
Work gloves

SOLAR STILL

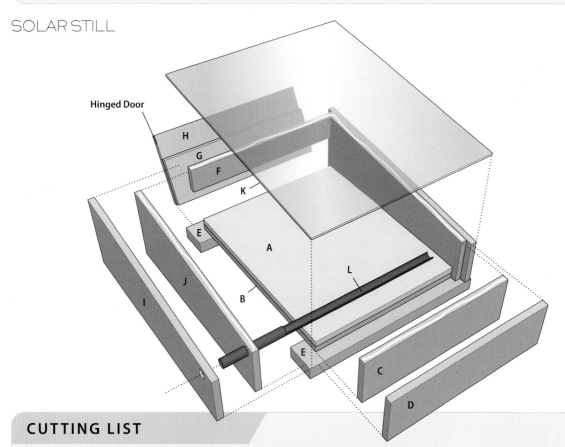

Hinged Door

CUTTING LIST

KEY	NUMBER	DIMENSION	MATERIAL
A	1	¾" × 23¾" × 19"	Rigid insulation
B	1	¾" × 23¾" × 19"	Plywood
C	1	¾" × 5¾" (high side) × 19"	Plywood
D	1	¾" × 5⅝" (high side) × 20½"	Plywood
E	2	1½" × 3½" × 22½"	2 × 4
F	1	¾" × 3" × 20½" (long to short edge)	Plywood
G	1	¾" × 5⅞" × 20½"	Plywood
H	1	¾" × 9" × 20½" (to long edge)	Plywood
I	2	¾" × 9⅛" × 5⅛" × 26¾"	Plywood
J	2	¾" × 8⅞" × 5⅝" × 24½"	Plywood
K	1	27¼" × 22" × ⅛"	Tempered glass
L	1	1"	PEX tubing, cut to length

☀ How to Build a Solar Still

1 Mark and cut the plywood pieces according to the cutting list, page 161. Cut the angled end pieces with a circular saw or tablesaw set to a 9° angle.

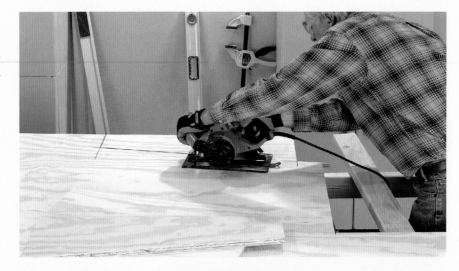

2 Cut the insulation the same size as the plywood base, then screw both to the 2 × 4 supports with 2½" screws.

1½"

1¾"

3 Screw the first layer of front and side pieces to the base and to each other, then add the back piece. Predrill the screws with a countersink bit.

4 Glue and screw the remaining front and side pieces on, using clamps to hold them together as you predrill and screw. Use 1¼" screws to laminate the pieces together and 2" screws to join the corners.

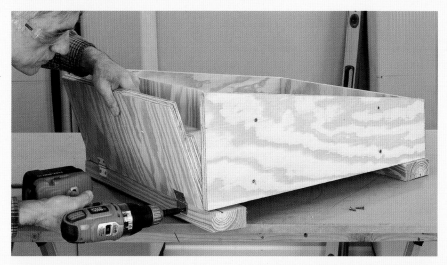

5 Glue and screw the hinged door pieces together, aligning the bottom and side edges, then set the door in position and screw on the hinges. Add a pull or knob at the center.

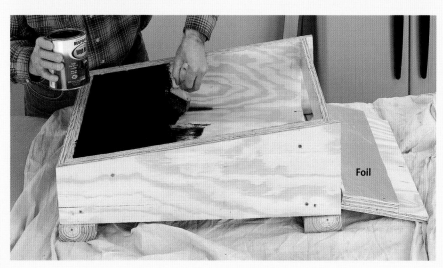

Foil

6 Paint the inside of the box with black high-temperature paint. Cover the back and the door with reflective foil glued with contact cement. Let the paint dry for several days so that all the solvents evaporate off.

continued on page 164

7 Apply weatherseal around the edges of the hinged door to make the door airtight.

8 Drill a hole for the PEX drain. The top of the PEX is ½" down from the top edge. Clamp a piece of scrap wood to the inside so the drill bit doesn't splinter the wood when it goes through.

9 Mark the first 19" of PEX, then cut it in half with a utility knife. Score it lightly at first to establish the cut lines.

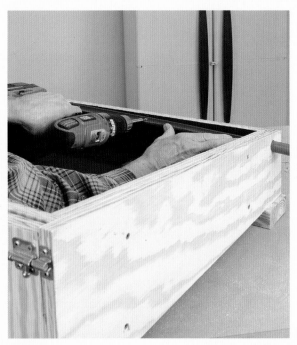

10 Drill three ⅛" holes in the side of the PEX for screws, then insert the PEX through the hole. Butt it tight against the other side, then screw it in place, sloping it about ¼".

11 Wipe a thick bead of silicone caulk along the top edge of the PEX to seal it against the plywood.

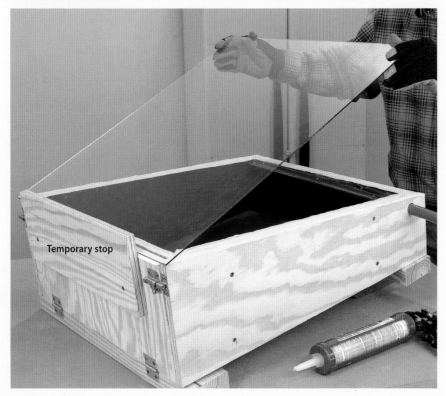

12 Shim the box level and tack a temporary stop to the top edge to make it easy to place the glass without smearing the caulk. Spread a generous bead of caulk on all the edges, then lay the glass in place. Tape it down around the edges with painter's tape, then let it set up overnight.

Temporary stop

Solar Lumber Kiln

For a woodworker, there's nothing like the thrill of cutting your own trees, milling and drying the rough-sawn planks, and then turning the best pieces into beautifully finished custom furniture. It's more work than just buying a few boards from the lumberyard, but there's a deep satisfaction to it that's hard to describe.

A critical part of the process is drying the wood so that it doesn't warp and crack after it's been made into furniture or flooring. Air drying will bring the wood to about a 20-percent moisture content, which is good enough for exterior use or rough work, but not enough for interior projects. Standard kilns use heaters and dehumidifiers to dry wood, but solar kilns are also being used successfully in all parts of the country, in both summer and winter, to dry wood down to a moisture content suitable for interior wood cabinets, paneling, and furniture—generally 7 to 10 percent. The black-painted interior of the kiln absorbs all the necessary heat from the sun, and a system of vents and fans removes the moisture. The fans can be solar powered, but the solar panels will need battery backup—the fans must stay on all day, then turn off at night to stop the wood from drying too quickly. (They may also need to be turned off when it rains or if the wood is drying unevenly.)

TOP LEFT
A solar kiln is ideal for a small-scale lumber mill or for woodworkers who mill their own wood.

LOWER LEFT
Fresh-cut hardwood from your own wood lot, such as this old-growth oak, has a special appeal. Drying these planks in a solar kiln helps bring out the character of the wood, without drying it so quickly that it cracks.

The ideal location for this kiln is a dry, well-ventilated area that gets at least five to six hours of direct, unshaded sun every day, year-round. Build the kiln so the side with the glazing faces due south, and make sure there's plenty of room in the back for the doors to swing open.

The kiln shown here is only 4 × 8 feet; this is large enough for lumber up to 6 feet in length and illustrates the basic construction. You can expand the size of the kiln as you need, as long as you have at least 1 square foot of glazing for every 10 board feet of lumber (one board foot is 1 foot × 1 foot × 1 inch thick), and leave 8 to 12 inches of space at the sides, front and back for air movement.

Our collector has roughly 40 square feet of glazing, so the maximum amount of wood we can put in it is 400 board feet.

Different wood species and thicknesses have different drying rates and need more or less heat and humidity, so it's a good idea to get a moisture meter and to do additional research on drying wood at the sites listed in the Resources (page 186). It's generally best to cut trees down in winter. Mill the tree into planks of lumber as soon as you can, then coat the ends with waterproofing or aluminum paint to keep the wood from drying unevenly. Stack it as soon as possible, with space between each board and ¾-inch slats between layers of boards, either in the kiln or under a roof.

Up to half the weight of a freshly cut tree may be water, and as this water evaporates the wood shrinks, cracks, and warps. Controlled drying of wood can minimize these problems and produce a larger number of solid, furniture-grade boards.

Solar kilns dry lumber as quickly and effectively as traditional kilns, but save money by using substantially less energy.

TOOLS & MATERIALS

Circular saw
Miter saw
Drill/driver with bits
Jigsaw
Hammer
Level
Stapler
Framing square
Tin snips
Clamps
¾" × 4 × 8 ext. grade plywood
½" × 4 × 8 treated plywood
⅜" × 4 × 8 T1-11 siding
⅜" × 4 × 8 ext. grade plywood
2 × 8 × 8 PT

2 × 4 × 12 (rafters)
1 × 4 × 8 cedar (corner trim)
1 × 4 × 10 cedar (corner trim)
1 × 4 × 12 cedar (corner trim)
1 × 6 × 12 cedar (roof trim)
Aluminum coil stock
Clear corrugated
  polycarbonate (two–12s
  or four–8s)
(2) Closure strips
  for polycarbonate
(2) Small window fans
2 × 6 joist hangers
(4) 3" to 4" metal angle
  (for corners)

10d framing nails (5 lb.)
10 galvanized framing nails
  (1 lb.)
Galvanized joist hanger nails
  (1 lb.)
1⅝" deck screws (5 lb.)
3" deck screws (1 lb.)
½" × 6 machine screws
Galvanized siding nails (5 lb.)
Neoprene washer screws (2 lb.)
Black silicone caulk
4-mil poly
2 × 6 × 15' fiberglass
  insulation (24' lineal)

2 × 4 × 15" fiberglass
  insulation (96' lineal)
Black rubber roofing paint
  (for inside walls)
Ext. paint and primer
Strap hinges (large size)
(4) Galvanized bolts
(4) 12" square louvre vents
Black silicone caulk
(4) 26 × 29"
  polycarbonate panels
Metal flashing (8 × 94½",
  14 × 97¼")
Eye and ear protection
Work gloves

SOLAR LUMBER KILN

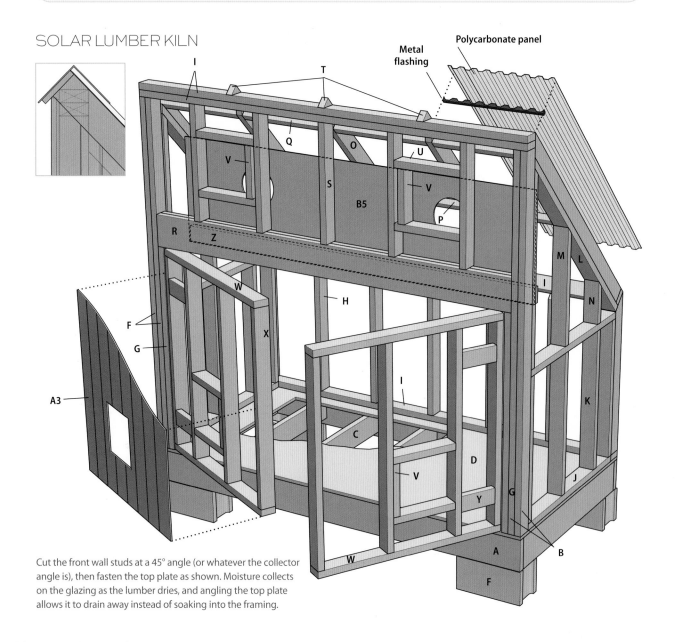

Cut the front wall studs at a 45° angle (or whatever the collector angle is), then fasten the top plate as shown. Moisture collects on the glazing as the lumber dries, and angling the top plate allows it to drain away instead of soaking into the framing.

FRAME CUTTING LIST

KEY	NUMBER	DIMENSION	PART	MATERIAL
A	2	1½" × 7¼" × 91½"	Rim joist	PT
B	2	1½" × 7¼" × 48"	Rim joist	PT
C	5	1½" × 5½" × 45"	Joists	SPF
D	1	¾" × 48" × 94½"	Floor	Plywood
E	1	½" × 45" × 91½"	Base	PT plywood
F	4	1½" × 3½" × 81"	Rear studs	SPF
G	2	1½" × 3½" × 48"	Rear cripples	SPF
H	7	1½" × 3½" × 38"	Front studs	SPF
I	4	1½" × 3½" × 94½"	Front and rear plates	SPF
J	4	1½" × 3½" × 41"	Lower side plates	SPF
K	8	1½" × 3½" × 33"	Lower side studs	SPF
L	2	1½" × 3½" × 59½"	Angled side plate	SPF
M	2	1½" × 3½" × 26"	Upper side stud	SPF
N	2	1½" × 3½" × 10"	Upper side stud	SPF
O	5	1½" × 3½" × 61⅜"	Rafters	SPF
P	4	1½" × 1½" × 21¾"	Blocking	SPF
Q	4	1½" × 3½" × 21¾"	Blocking	SPF
R	2	1½" × 7¼" × 88½"	Rear wall header	SPF
S	7	1½" × 3½" × 26"	Rear studs	SPF
T	3	2½" × 2½" × 3½"	Triangular support blocks	SPF
U	8	1½" × 3½" × 14½"	Vent blocking	SPF
V	4	1½" × 3½" × 12¼"	Vertical vent blocking	SPF
W	4	1½" × 3½" × 42½"	Door top and bottom	SPF
X	8	1½" × 3½" × 44½"	Door studs	SPF
Y	4	1½" × 3½" × 8¼"	Hinge backer	SPF
Z	1	1½" × 3½" × 86¾"	Fan shroud support	SPF
Z1	2	1½" × 3½" × 22"	Fan shroud nailer	SPF

EXTERIOR SIDING CUTTING LIST (USE ANY EXTERIOR GRADE SIDING)

KEY	NUMBER	DIMENSION	PART
A1	1	47" × 94½" W	Front
A2	2	95½" × 48" W	Sides
A3	2	47½" × 42½" W	Door
A4	2	91" × 47¼" W	Rear

TRIM (ROUGH-SAWN CEDAR)

KEY	NUMBER	DIMENSION	PART
C1	1	¾" × 3½" × 95¾"	Front
C2	1	¾" × 5½" × 97¼"	Top
C3	2	¾" × 3½" × 69¾"	Diagonal sides
C4	2	¾" × 3½" × 43"	Front
C5	2	¾" × 2½" × 44½"	Front sides
C6	2	¾" × 3½" × 92¼"	Rear
C7	2	¾" × 2½" × 91¾"	Rear sides
C8	1	¾" × 3½" × 46"	Door astragal
C9	1	¾" × 3½" × 12"	Door stop

INTERIOR SIDING CUTTING LIST (⅜" PLYWOOD)

KEY	NUMBER	DIMENSION	PART	MATERIAL
A	2	¾" × 64" × 19"	Sides	Plywood
B	2	¾" × 24⁷⁄₁₆" × 7½"	Ends	Plywood
C	2	1½" × 1½" × 25⅞"	Stops	2 × 2
D	2	¾" × 2½" × 48"	Side nailers	1 × 3
E	1	¾" × 2½" × 20¾"	End nailer	1 × 3
F	1	¼" × 46" × 24½"	Back	Plywood
G	1	¼" × 10" × 24½"	Upper back	Plywood
H	1	¼" × 44" × 22½"	Divider	Plywood
I	1	¼" × 14¼" × 22½"	Upper divider	Plywood
J	2	¾" × 2½" × 14"	Upper nailer	1 × 3
K	1	¾" × 10¼" × 25⅞"	Top cap	Plywood
L	1	¾" × 7¼" × 25⅞"	Top door	1 × 8
M	1	¾" × 4" × 25⅞"	Bottom door	1 × 6
N	1	52" × 25⅞"	Glazing	Polycarbonate
O	2	1½" × 1½" × 53"	Corners	Aluminum
P	2	¾" × 3½" × 25½"	Side brace	1 × 4 PT
Q	1	1½" × 3½" × 25⅞"	Back brace	2 × 4 PT
R	1	44" × 22½"	Heat absorber	Aluminum

☀ Solar Lumber Kiln: How to Build the Frame

1 Level a base of treated wood or concrete blocks at the kiln location, then build the frame for the floor on top of them. The kiln should be built in a south-facing location that gets at least five to six hours of direct sunlight.

2 Flip the framework over, then screw ½" treated plywood to the underside of the frame. Caulk all the edges to prevent ants and other insects from colonizing the base.

3 Turn the frame right-side up again. Fill the cavities with insulation (use kraft-faced or add a vapor barrier). Screw the ¾" plywood to the joists with 1⅝" deck screws.

4 Frame the front and rear walls, then stand them up on the platform. Screw them in place, then level and brace the rear wall.

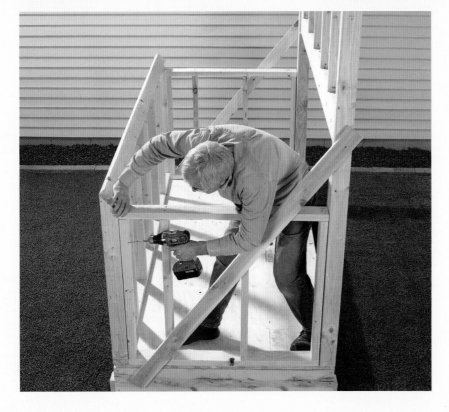

5 Build the half-walls for the sides, then fit them in and screw them to the front and back walls.

continued on page 174

6 Nail the exterior siding to the framing for the front wall. The top edge should be lower than the top of the 2 × 4 framing to leave room for the glazing overhang. Nail temporary stops at the corner to help position the siding.

7 Insulate the front wall, then add the vapor barrier and the ⅜" interior plywood siding. Leave the plywood ⅜ to ½" short of the top plate.

8 Nail the coil stock to the top plate, leaving a 3" overhang on each side. Screw a 2 × 4 over the coil stock, matching the top plate position, then bend the coil stock over the edges and nail it in place. (Gutter repair tape or a strip of EPDM roofing can be used instead of coil stock.)

9 Measure and cut the rafters. Lay out the rafters 24" on center, starting with the center rafter and working to the sides, so that the overhang at the edges will be equal. Check the rafter layout against the polycarbonate panels to make sure they line up properly. Note that the panels are fastened through the crowns, rather than in the valleys.

10 Fill in the framing for the angled part of the sides.

11 Frame the rear doors. Make sure that the doors are ½" less than the height of the opening and ½" less (total) than the opening width. Frame openings for the vents, and add a hinge backer.

continued on page 176

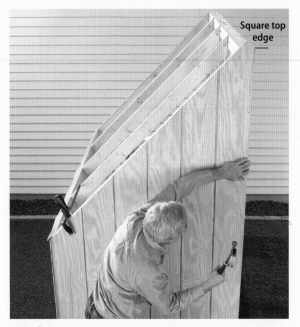

12 Install exterior siding on the walls and doors and above and below the doors. Square off the top end of the side piece as shown so it lines up with the 2 × 4 top plate and creates a small roof profile.

Square top edge

13 Screw the strap hinges to the doors at the 2 × 4 backer locations. Shim the doors so they're tight and evenly spaced in the opening, with the door against the frame, then screw the hinges to the frame. Drive just one screw into each hinge at first, then remove the shims and check the fit. Adjust if necessary when you drive the rest of the screws in.

14 Add insulation to the walls and doors, staple on the vapor barrier, then nail on the interior plywood siding.

15 Attach crosspieces between the rafters to stiffen and support the glazing panels. Screw them in through the backs of the rafters at an angle.

16 Cut the shroud that the fans are attached to from ⅜" or ½" plywood. Attach 2 × 4 nailers to the sides (hidden behind the shroud in this photo), and screw a 2 × 4 across the bottom. Make cutouts for the fans you buy, then hang the shroud from the rafters with hurricane ties and screw the 2 × 4 to the side walls. (Fans can be any inexpensive type, 8" to 14" round or square, as long as you can find a way to fasten them.)

17 Fasten the fans to the shroud. The fans are turned on during the day to circulate the air, then turned off at night so the wood doesn't dry too quickly, so they should be plugged into a timer.

18 Form the top of the kiln by extending the 1 × 4 diagonal trim to the edge of the framing, then join the two sides of the kiln with a 1 × 6 cap. Nail on triangular blocks for nailers and to help support the peak of the roof.

19 Paint all of the interior with black roofing paint. Caulk all the corners with black silicone after the paint dries. Paint or stain the exterior whatever color you wish, but use acrylic latex so any trapped moisture can escape.

continued on page 178

20 Align the four polycarbonate panels, then clamp the ends with spring clamps and mark the cut line. Place 2 × 4s under both sides of the cut, then place cardboard or plywood on top, under the circular saw, so the panel doesn't get scratched. Use a sharp plywood-cutting blade (or whatever blade the panel instructions recommend) to cut the panels.

21 Set the panels in position over the foam closure strips, then predrill the holes on the crowns. Use a sharp bit ⅛" bigger than the diameter of the neoprene screw to allow for movement. Don't overtighten the screws—they should be tight against the panel, but should not distort it.

22 Cut a 14"-wide piece of sheet-metal or aluminum coil stock slightly longer than the roof, then bend it at the center to create a cap for the roof. Drill holes through the metal, polycarbonate, and closure strips in the front, then fasten with neoprene screws into the blocking. Screw the metal to the 1 × 6 in back.

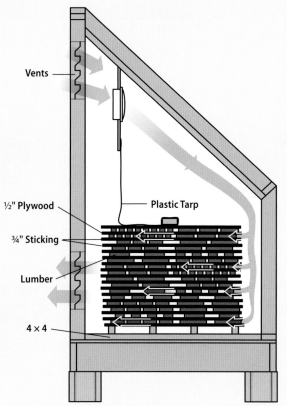

Stack the lumber on ¾" sticking spaced every 16", with several 4 × 4s at the bottom. Paint a piece of plywood black and set it on top of the stack to shield the lumber from direct sun. Hang a 6 × 8' dark plastic tarp from screws on the bottom of the shroud (drive screws at the grommet locations), then staple and wrap the other end around a 7'-long 2 × 4 and set it on the plywood. The tarp will help channel the air from the fan through the stacked lumber. As the warm air circulates, moisture is gradually exhausted through the vents. If you need to lower temperatures during the drying process, you can cover part of the glazing with a tarp. Leave the glazing covered or open the back when the kiln is not in use—the temperatures can get high enough to warp plastic fan blades.

Glossary

III-V cell — A high-efficiency solar cell composed of materials from the periodic table.

AC — See alternating current.

Activated shelf life — The period of time at a specific temperature that a charged battery can be stored before its capacity plummets to unusable levels.

Activation voltage(s) — The voltage(s) at which charge controller engage to protect the batteries.

Adjustable set point — A feature allowing the user to change the voltage levels at which a charge controller becomes active.

Alternating current (AC) — A type of electrical current, the direction of which is reversed at regular intervals or cycles. In the United States, the standard is 120 reversals or 60 cycles per second. Electricity transmission networks use AC because voltage can be controlled with relative ease.

Ambient temperature — The temperature of the surrounding area.

Amperage Interrupt Capability (AIC) — direct current fuses should be rated with a sufficient AIC to interrupt the highest possible current flowing through the system.

Ampere (amp) — The basic unit of electrical current (or rate of flow of electrons). One volt across one ohm of resistance causes a current flow of one ampere.

Ampere-hour (Ah/AH) — A measure of the flow of current over one hour; used to measure battery capacity.

ampere hour meter — A tool that monitors current with time. The indication is the product of current (in amperes) and time (in hours).

Angle of incidence — The angle from a ray of sun to line perpendicular to the surface. For example, a surface that directly faces the sun has a solar angle of incidence of zero. If the surface is parallel to the sun (sunrise striking a horizontal rooftop), the angle of incidence is 90°.

Anode — The positive electrode of a battery. Also, the earth or ground in a cathodic protection system. Also, the positive terminal of a diode.

Array current — The electrical current produced by a photovoltaic array when exposed to sunlight.

Array operating voltage — The voltage produced by a photovoltaic array when exposed to sunlight and connected to a load.

Azimuth angle — The angle between true south and the point on the horizon directly below the sun.

Base load — The average amount of electric power that a utility is required to supply in any period.

Battery — Two or more electrochemical cells enclosed in a container and electrically interconnected in a functional series/parallel arrangement to provide the required operating voltage and current levels. Under common usage, the term *battery* also applies to a single cell if it constitutes the entire electrochemical storage system.

Battery available capacity — The total maximum charge (expressed in ampere-hours) that can be withdrawn from a cell or battery under a specific set of operating conditions, including temperature, discharge rate, initial state of charge, age of battery, and cut-off voltage.

Battery capacity — The maximum total electrical charge (expressed in ampere-hours) which a battery can deliver to a load under a specific set of conditions.

Battery cell — The simplest operating unit in a storage battery. It consists of one or more positive electrodes or plates, an electrolyte that permits ionic conduction, one or more negative electrodes or plates, separators between plates of opposite polarity, and a container for all the above.

Battery energy capacity — The total energy available, expressed in watt-hours (kilowatt-hours), which can be withdrawn from a fully charged cell or battery.

Battery life — The period during which a cell or battery is capable of operating above a specified capacity or efficiency performance level. Life may be measured in cycles and/ or years.

British thermal unit (BTU) — The amount of heat required to raise the temperature of one pound of water one degree Fahrenheit; equal to 252 calories.

Capacity (C) — See battery capacity.

Cathode — The negative pole or electrode of an electrolytic cell where electrons enter (current leaves) the system; the opposite of an anode.

Cell (battery) — A single unit of an electrochemical device capable of producing direct voltage by converting chemical energy into electrical energy. A battery usually consists of several cells electrically connected together to produce higher voltages.

Charge — The process of adding electrical energy to a battery.

Charge controller — A component of a photovoltaic system that controls the flow of current to and from the battery to protect it from over-charge and over-discharge. The charge controller may also indicate the system operational status.

Charge rate — The current applied to a cell or battery to restore its available capacity. This rate is commonly normalized by a charge control device with respect to the rated capacity of the cell or battery.

Cloud enhancement — The increase in solar intensity caused by reflected irradiance from nearby clouds.

Combined collector — A photovoltaic device or module that provides heat energy in addition to electricity.

Conduction band (or conduction level) — An energy band in a semiconductor in which electrons can move freely in a solid, producing a net transport of charge.

Conductor — The material through which electricity is transmitted, such as an electrical wire.

Converter — A unit that converts a direct current (dc) voltage to another dc voltage.

Current — See electric current.

Current at maximum power (Imp) — The current at which maximum power is available from a module.

Cutoff voltage — The voltage levels (activation) at which the charge controller disconnects the photovoltaic array from the battery or the load from the battery.

Cycle — The discharge and subsequent charge of a battery.

Days of storage — The number of consecutive days the stand-alone system will meet a defined load without solar energy input. This term is related to system availability.

DC — See direct current.

Demand response — The process of using voluntary load reductions during peak hours.

Diffuse insolation — Sunlight received indirectly as a result of scattering due to clouds, fog, haze, dust, or other obstructions in the atmosphere. Opposite of direct insolation.

Diffuse radiation — Radiation received from the sun after reflection and scattering by the atmosphere and ground.

Diode — An electronic device that allows current to flow in one direction only. See also blocking diode and bypass diode.

Direct current (DC) — A type of electricity transmission and distribution by which electricity flows in one direction through the conductor, usually relatively low voltage and high current. To be used for typical 120-volt or 220-volt household appliances, DC must be converted to alternating current, its opposite.

Direct insolation — Sunlight falling directly upon a collector. Opposite of diffuse insolation.

Discharge — The withdrawal of electrical energy from a battery.

Discharge rate — The rate, usually expressed in amperes or time, at which electrical current is taken from the battery.

Disconnect — Switch gear used to connect or disconnect components in a photovoltaic system.

Distributed generation — A popular term for localized or on-site power generation.

Distributed power — Generic term for any power supply located near the point where the power is used. Opposite of central power. See also stand-alone systems.

Distributed systems — Systems that are installed at or near the location where the electricity is used, as opposed to central systems that supply electricity to grids. A residential photovoltaic system is a distributed system.

Downtime — Time when the photovoltaic system cannot provide power for the load. Usually expressed in hours per year or that percentage.

Dry cell — A cell (battery) with a captive electrolyte. A primary battery that cannot be recharged.

Duty cycle — The ratio of active time to total time. Used to describe the operating regime of appliances or loads in photovoltaic systems.

Duty rating — The amount of time an inverter (power conditioning unit) can produce at full rated power.

Electric circuit — The path followed by electrons from a power source (generator or battery), through an electrical system, and returning to the source.

Electric current — The flow of electrical energy (electricity) in a conductor, measured in amperes.

Electrical grid — An integrated system of electricity distribution.

Electricity — Energy resulting from the flow of charge particles, such as electrons or ions.

Electrochemical cell — A device containing two conducting electrodes, one positive and the other negative, made of dissimilar materials (usually metals) that are immersed in a chemical solution (electrolyte) that transmits positive ions from the negative to the positive electrode and thus forms an electrical charge. One or more cells constitute a battery.

Electrode — A conductor that is brought in conducting contact with a ground.

Energy — The capability of doing work; different forms of energy can be converted to other forms, but the total amount of energy remains the same.

Energy audit — A survey that shows how much energy you use in your home, and which will help you determine how to use less energy.

Equinox — The two times of year when the sun crosses the equator and night and day are roughly the same amount of time. The spring equinox occurs on March 20 or 21 (spring equinox) and the fall equinox occurs on September 22 or 23.

Fixed-tilt array — A photovoltaic array set at a fixed angle with respect to horizontal.

Flat-plate array — A photovoltaic array that consists of non-concentrating PV modules.

Flat-plate module — An arrangement of photovoltaic cells or material mounted on a rigid flat surface with the cells exposed freely to incoming sunlight.

Full sun — The amount of power density in sunlight hitting the earth's surface at noon on a clear day (about 1,000 Watts/square meter).

Gigawatt (GW) — A unit of power equal to 1 billion watts; 1 million kilowatts, or 1,000 megawatts.

Grid — See electrical grid.

Grid-connected system — A solar electric or photovoltaic (PV) system in which the PV array acts like a central generating plant and supplies power to the grid.

Grid-interactive system — Same as grid-connected system.

Grid lines — Metallic contacts fused to the surface of the solar cell to provide a low resistance path for electrons to flow out to the cell interconnect wires.

High-voltage disconnect — The voltage at which a charge controller will disconnect the photovoltaic array from the batteries to prevent overcharging.

Hybrid system — A solar electric or photovoltaic system that includes other sources of electricity generation, such as wind or diesel generators.

Incident light — Light that shines onto the face of a solar cell or module.

Input voltage — Determined by the total power required by the alternating current loads and the voltage of any direct current loads. Generally, the larger the load, the higher the inverter input voltage. This keeps the current at levels where switches and other components are readily available.

Interconnect — A conductor within a module or other means of connection that provides an electrical interconnection between the solar cells.

Inverter — A device that converts direct current electricity to alternating current either for stand-alone systems or to supply power to an electricity grid.

Irradiance — The direct, diffuse, and reflected solar radiation that strikes a surface, usually expressed in kilowatts per square meter.

ISPRA guidelines — Guidelines for the assessment of photovoltaic power plants, published by the Joint Research Centre of the Commission of the European Communities, Ispra, Italy.

Joule — A metric unit of energy or work; 1 joule per second equals 1 watt or 0.737 foot-pounds; 1 BTU equals 1,055 joules.

Kilowatt (kW) — A standard unit of electrical power equal to 1000 watts, or to the energy consumption at a rate of 1000 joules per second.

Kilowatt-hour (kWh) — 1,000 watts acting over a period of 1 hour. The kWh is a unit of energy. 1 kWh=3600 kJ.

Lead-acid battery — A general category that includes batteries with plates made of pure lead, lead-antimony, or lead-calcium immersed in an acid electrolyte.

Life — The period during which a system is capable of operating above a specified performance level.

Life-cycle cost — The estimated cost of owning and operating a photovoltaic system for the period of its useful life.

Light trapping — The trapping of light inside a semiconductor material by refracting and reflecting the light at critical angles; trapped light travels further within the material, greatly increasing the probability of absorption and hence of producing charge carriers.

Liquid electrolyte battery — A battery containing a liquid solution of acid and water. Distilled water may be added to these batteries to replenish the electrolyte as necessary (also known as a *flooded battery* because the plates are covered with the electrolyte.

Load — The demand on an energy producing system; the energy consumption or requirement of a piece or group of equipment. Usually expressed in terms of amperes or watts in reference to electricity.

Load circuit — The fuses, wires, switches, etc. that connect the load to the power source.

Low-voltage cutoff (LVC) — The voltage level at which a charge controller will disconnect the load from the battery.

Low-voltage disconnect — The voltage at which a charge controller will disconnect the load from the batteries to prevent over-discharging.

Low-voltage warning — A warning buzzer or light that indicates the low battery voltage set point has been reached.

Maintenance-free battery — A sealed battery to which water cannot be added to maintain the recommended electrolyte level.

Megawatt (MW) — 1,000 kilowatts, or 1 million watts; standard measure of electric powerplant generating capacity.

Megawatt-hour — 1,000 kilowatt-hours or 1 million watt-hours.

Micrometer (micron) — One millionth of a meter.

Module — See photovoltaic (PV) module.

Multi-stage controller — A charging controller unit that allows different charging currents as the battery nears its full state of charge.

Nanometer — One billionth of a meter.

National Electrical Code (NEC) — Contains guidelines for all types of electrical installations. The 1984 and later editions of the NEC contain Article 690, "Solar Photovoltaic Systems," which should be followed when installing a PV system.

National Electrical Manufacturers Association (NEMA) — This organization sets standards for some non-electronic products like junction boxes.

NEC — See National Electrical Code.

NEMA — See National Electrical Manufacturers Association.

Nominal voltage — A reference voltage used to describe batteries, modules, or systems (i.e., a 12-volt or 24-volt battery, module, or system).

Ohm — A measure of the electrical resistance of a material equal to the resistance of a circuit in which the potential difference of 1 volt produces a current of 1 ampere.

Open-circuit voltage (Voc) — The maximum possible voltage across a photovoltaic cell; the voltage across the cell in sunlight when no current is flowing.

Operating point — The current and voltage that a photovoltaic module or array produces when connected to a load. The operating point is dependent on the load or the batteries connected to the output terminals of the array.

Overcharge — Forcing current into a fully charged battery. The battery will be damaged if overcharged for a long period.

Panel — See photovoltaic panel.

Parallel connection — A way of joining solar cells or photovoltaic modules by connecting positive leads together and negative leads together, increasing the current but not the voltage.

Peak sun hours — The equivalent number of hours per day when solar irradiance averages 1,000 w/m2. For example, six peak sun hours means that the energy received during total daylight hours equals the energy that would have been received had the irradiance for six hours been 1,000 w/m2.

Photoelectric cell — A device for measuring light intensity that works by converting light falling on it to electricity, and then measuring the current; used in photometers.

Photon — A particle of light that acts as an individual unit of energy.

Photovoltaic(s) (PV) — Pertaining to the direct conversion of light into electricity.

Photovoltaic (PV) array — An interconnected system of PV modules that function as a single electricity-producing unit. The modules are assembled as a discrete structure, with common support or mounting. In smaller systems, an array can consist of a single module.

Photovoltaic (PV) cell — The smallest semiconductor element within a PV module to perform the immediate conversion of light into electrical energy (direct current voltage and current). Also called a solar cell.

Photovoltaic (PV) conversion efficiency — The ratio of the electric power produced by a photovoltaic device to the power of the sunlight incident on the device.

Photovoltaic (PV) device — A solid-state electrical device that converts light directly into direct current electricity.

Photovoltaic (PV) module — The smallest environmentally protected, essentially planar assembly of solar cells and ancillary parts, such as interconnections, terminals, (and protective devices such as diodes) intended to generate direct current power under unconcentrated sunlight. The structural (load carrying) member of a module can either be the top layer (superstrate) or the back layer (substrate).

Photovoltaic (PV) panel — often used interchangeably with PV module (especially in one-module systems), but more accurately used to refer to a physically connected collection of modules (i.e., a laminate string of modules used to achieve a required voltage and current).

Photovoltaic (PV) system — A complete set of components for converting sunlight into electricity by the photovoltaic process.

Plates — A metal plate, usually lead or lead compound, immersed in the electrolyte in a battery.

Plug-and-play PV system — A commercial, off-the-shelf photovoltaic system that is fully inclusive with little need for individual customization. The system can be installed without special training and using few tools. The homeowner plugs the system into a PV-ready circuit and an automatic PV discovery process initiates communication between the system and the utility. The system and grid are automatically configured for optimal operation.

Power — The amount of electrical energy available for doing work, measured in horsepower, watts, or BTUs per hour.

Primary battery — A battery whose initial capacity cannot be restored by charging.

PV — See photovoltaic(s).

Ramp — A change in generation output.

Ramp rate — The ability of a generating unit to change its output over some unit of time, often measured in MW/min.

Rated battery capacity — The term used by battery manufacturers to indicate the maximum amount of energy that can be withdrawn from a battery under specified discharge rate and temperature. See also battery capacity.

Rectifier — A device that converts alternating current to direct current. See also inverter.

Regulator — Prevents overcharging of batteries by controlling charge cycle—usually adjustable to conform to specific battery needs.

Remote systems — See stand-alone systems.

Reserve capacity — The amount of generating capacity a central power system must maintain to meet peak loads.

Resistance (R) — The property of a conductor, which opposes the flow of an electric current resulting in the generation of heat in the conducting material. The measure of the resistance of a given conductor is the electromotive force needed for a unit current flow. The unit of resistance is ohms.

Reverse current protection — Any method of preventing unwanted current flow from the battery to the photovoltaic array (usually at night). See also blocking diode.

Sealed battery — A battery with a captive electrolyte and a resealing vent cap, also called a valve-regulated battery. Electrolyte cannot be added.

Secondary battery — A battery that can be recharged.

Self-discharge — The rate at which a battery, without a load, will lose its charge.

Series connection — A way of joining photovoltaic cells by connecting positive leads to negative leads, increasing the voltage.

Series controller — A charge controller that interrupts the charging current by open-circuiting the photovoltaic (PV) array. The control element is in series with the PV array and battery.

Series regulator — Type of battery charge regulator where the charging current is controlled by a switch connected in series with the photovoltaic module or array.

Shallow-cycle battery — A battery with small plates that cannot withstand many discharges to a low state-of-charge.

Short-circuit current (Isc) — The current flowing freely through an external circuit that lacks and resistance; the maximum current possible.

Single-stage controller — A charge controller that redirects all charging current as the battery nears full state-of-charge.

Smart grid — An intelligent electric power system that regulates the two-way flow of electricity and information between power plants and consumers to control grid activity.

Solar cell — See photovoltaic (PV) cell.

Solar constant — The average amount of solar radiation that reaches the earth's upper atmosphere on a surface perpendicular to the sun's rays; equal to 1,353 watts per square meter or 492 BTU per square foot.

Solar cooling — The use of solar thermal energy or solar electricity to power a cooling appliance. Photovoltaic systems can power evaporative coolers ("swamp" coolers), heat-pumps, and air conditioners.

Solar energy — Electromagnetic energy transmitted from the sun (solar radiation). The amount that reaches the earth is equal to one billionth of total solar energy generated, or the equivalent of about 420 trillion kilowatt-hours.

Solar noon — The time of the day, at a specific location, when the sun reaches its highest, apparent point in the sky.

Solar panel — See photovoltaic (PV) panel.

Solar resource — The amount of solar insolation a site receives, usually measured in kWh/m2/day, which is equivalent to the number of peak sun hours.

Solar spectrum — The total distribution of electromagnetic radiation emanating from the sun. The different regions of the solar spectrum are described by their wavelength range.

Solar thermal electric systems — Solar energy conversion technologies that convert solar energy to electricity, by heating a working fluid to power a turbine that drives a generator. Examples of these systems include central receiver systems, parabolic dish, and solar trough.

Specific gravity — The ratio of the weight of the solution to the weight of an equal volume of water at a specified temperature. Used as an indicator of battery state-of-charge.

Split-spectrum cell — A compound photovoltaic device in which sunlight is first divided into spectral regions by optical means. Each region is then directed to a different photovoltaic cell optimized for converting that portion of the spectrum into electricity. Such a device achieves significantly greater overall conversion of incident sunlight into electricity.

Stand-alone system — An autonomous or hybrid photovoltaic system not connected to a grid.

Standby current — The amount of current (power) used by the inverter when no load is active (lost power). When load demand is low, the efficiency of the inverter is lowest.

Stand-off mounting — Technique for mounting a photovoltaic array on a sloped roof, which involves mounting the modules a short distance above the pitched roof and tilting them to the optimum angle.

State-of-charge (SOC) — The available capacity remaining in the battery, expressed as a percentage of the rated capacity.

String — A number of photovoltaic panels or modules interconnected electrically in series to produce the operating voltage required by the load.

Subsystem — Any one of several components in a photovoltaic system, such as a controller, array, battery, or inverter.

Surge capacity — The maximum power, usually 3-5 times the rated power, that can be provided over a short time.

System availability — The percentage of time (usually expressed in hours per year) when a photovoltaic system will be able to fully meet the load demand.

System operating voltage — The photovoltaic array output voltage under load. The system operating voltage is dependent on the load or batteries connected to the output terminals.

Tilt angle — The angle at which a photovoltaic array is set to face the sun relative to a horizontal position. The tilt angle can be set or adjusted to maximize seasonal or annual energy collection.

Total AC load demand — The total of the alternating current loads. This value is important when selecting an inverter.

Tracking array — A photovoltaic array that follows the path of the sun to maximize the solar radiation incident on the PV surface. The two most common orientations are (1), one axis where the array tracks the sun east to west; and (2), two-axis tracking where the array points directly at the sun at all times. Tracking arrays use both the direct and diffuse sunlight. Two-axis tracking arrays capture the maximum possible daily energy.

Trickle charge — A charge at a low rate, balancing through self-discharge losses, to maintain a cell or battery in a fully charged condition.

Two-axis tracking — A photovoltaic array tracking system capable of rotating independently about two axes (e.g., vertical and horizontal).

Utility-interactive inverter — An inverter that can function only when tied to the utility grid, and uses the prevailing line-voltage frequency on the utility line as a control parameter to ensure that the photovoltaic system's output is fully synchronized with the utility power.

Varistor — A voltage-dependent variable resistor. Normally used to protect sensitive equipment from power spikes or lightning strikes by shunting the energy to ground.

Volt (V) — A unit of electrical force equal to that amount of electromotive force that will cause a steady current of one ampere to flow through a resistance of one ohm.

Voltage — The amount of electromotive force, measured in volts, that exists between two points.

Voltage at maximum power (Vmp) — The voltage at which maximum power is available from a photovoltaic module.

Voltage protection — Many inverters have sensing circuits that will disconnect the unit from the battery if input voltage limits are exceeded.

Voltage regulation — This indicates the variability in the output voltage. Some loads will not tolerate voltage variations greater than a few percent.

Watt — The rate of energy transfer equivalent to one ampere under an electrical pressure of one volt. One watt equals 1/746 horsepower, or one joule per second. It is the product of voltage and current (amperage).

Zenith angle — the angle between the direction of interest (of the sun, for example) and the zenith (directly overhead).

Resources

GUIDE TO FEDERAL, STATE AND LOCAL INCENTIVES

DSIRE – Database of State Incentives for Renewables and Efficiency
www.dsireusa.org

GENERAL INFORMATION ABOUT SOLAR ENERGY

ASES—American Solar Energy Society
www.ases.org

Build It Solar
www.builditsolar.com

Find My Shadow (solar position charts)
www.findmyshadow.com

Florida Solar Energy Center
www.fsec.ucf.edu/en

Home Power Magazine
www.homepower.com/home

PVWatts (National Renewable Energy Laboratory's energy production & cost calculator)
pvwatts.nrel.gov

SEIA (Solar Energy Industries Association)
www.seia.org

US Dept. of Energy
www.energysavers.gov

SOLAR ENERGY PRODUCTS AND MATERIALS

Applied Energy Innovations
(612)-532-0384
www.appliedenergyinnovations.org

Backwoods Solar
(208)-263-4290
www.backwoodssolar.com

Enphase
(877)-797-4743
www.enphase.com

Itron
(510)-844-2800
www.itron.com

Midnite Solar Inc.
(360)-403-7207
www.midnitesolar.com

Morningstar Solar
(215)-321-4457
www.morningstarcorp.com

Northern Arizona Wind and Sun
(800)-383-0195
www.windsun.com

Silicon Solar
(800)-789-0329
www.siliconsolar.com

SolarEdge
(510)-498-3200
www.solaredge.com

Real Goods
(800)-919-2400
www.realgoods.com

Sundance Solar
(603)-225-2020
www.sundancesolar.com

Zilla Corporation
(720)-880-6700
www.zillarac.com

MOUNTING SYSTEMS

Unistrut
www.unistrut.org

Unirac
www.unirac.com

Thompson Technology
(415)-166-0103
www.thompsontec.com

QuickMount PV
www.quickmountpv.com

SOLAR COOKING

Solar Cookers International
www.solarcooking.org

Solar Cooker-at-Cantinawest
www.solarcooker-at-cantinawest.com

Solar Oven Society
www.solarovens.org

Cook With The Sun
www.cookwiththesun.com

SOLAR HOT WATER

U.P. Solar Solutions
(888)-744-8797
www.aluminum-solar-absorbers.com

SOLAR REFLECTIVE FOILS

Clear Dome Solar Thermal
(619)-990-7977
www.cleardomesolar.com

SOLAR AIR HEATERS

Environmental Solar Systems
(978)-975-1190
www.sunmatesolarpanels.com

Your Solar Home
(866)-556-5504
www.yoursolarhome.com

POLYCARBONATE PANELS

Tuftex
(800)-777-7663
www.tuftexpanel.com

Greenhouse Megastore
(888)-281-9337
www.greenhousemegastore.com

Advance Greenhouses
(877)-238-8357
www.advancegreenhouses.com

SOLAR KILN

U.S. Forest Products Laboratory
www.fpl.fs.fed.us

Virginia Tech
www.woodsciencevt.edu/about/extention/vtsolar_kiln

Photo Credits

Conversions

Metric Equivalent

	1/64	1/32	1/25	1/16	1/8	1/4	3/8	2/5	1/2	5/8	3/4	7/8	1	2	3	4	5	6	7	8	9	10	11	12	36	39.4
Inches (in.)	1/64	1/32	1/25	1/16	1/8	1/4	3/8	2/5	1/2	5/8	3/4	7/8	1	2	3	4	5	6	7	8	9	10	11	12	36	39.4
Feet (ft.)																								1	3	3 1/12
Yards (yd.)																									1	1 1/12
Millimeters (mm)	0.40	0.79	1	1.59	3.18	6.35	9.53	10	12.7	15.9	19.1	22.2	25.4	50.8	76.2	101.6	127	152	178	203	229	254	279	305	914	1,000
Centimeters (cm)							0.95	1	1.27	1.59	1.91	2.22	2.54	5.08	7.62	10.16	12.7	15.2	17.8	20.3	22.9	25.4	27.9	30.5	91.4	100
Meters (m)																								.30	.91	1.00

Converting Measurements

To Convert:	To:	Multiply by:
Inches	Millimeters	25.4
Inches	Centimeters	2.54
Feet	Meters	0.305
Yards	Meters	0.914
Miles	Kilometers	1.609
Square inches	Square centimeters	6.45
Square feet	Square meters	0.093
Square yards	Square meters	0.836
Cubic inches	Cubic centimeters	16.4
Cubic feet	Cubic meters	0.0283
Cubic yards	Cubic meters	0.765
Pints (US)	Liters	0.473 (Imp. 0.568)
Quarts (US)	Liters	0.946 (Imp. 1.136)
Gallons (US)	Liters	3.785 (Imp. 4.546)
Ounces	Grams	28.4
Pounds	Kilograms	0.454
Tons	Metric tons	0.907

To Convert:	To:	Multiply by:
Millimeters	Inches	0.039
Centimeters	Inches	0.394
Meters	Feet	3.28
Meters	Yards	1.09
Kilometers	Miles	0.621
Square centimeters	Square inches	0.155
Square meters	Square feet	10.8
Square meters	Square yards	1.2
Cubic centimeters	Cubic inches	0.061
Cubic meters	Cubic feet	35.3
Cubic meters	Cubic yards	1.31
Liters	Pints (US)	2.114 (Imp. 1.76)
Liters	Quarts (US)	1.057 (Imp. 0.88)
Liters	Gallons (US)	0.264 (Imp. 0.22)
Grams	Ounces	0.035
Kilograms	Pounds	2.2
Metric tons	Tons	1.1

Converting Temperatures

Convert degrees Fahrenheit (F) to degrees Celsius (C) by following this simple formula: Subtract 32 from the Fahrenheit temperature reading. Then mulitply that number by 5/9. For example, 77°F - 32 = 45. 45 × 5/9 = 25°C.

To convert degrees Celsius to degrees Fahrenheit, multiply the Celsius temperature reading by 9/5, then add 32. For example, 25°C × 9/5 = 45. 45 + 32 = 77°F.

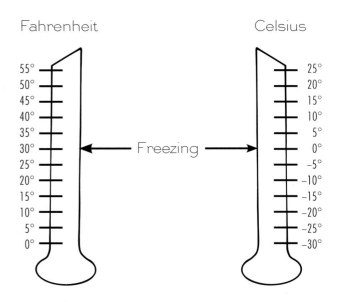

Fahrenheit — Celsius

Freezing

Drill Bit Guide

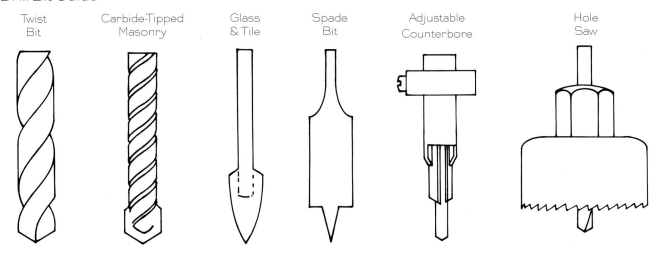

Twist Bit   Carbide-Tipped Masonry   Glass & Tile   Spade Bit   Adjustable Counterbore   Hole Saw

Nails

Nail lengths are identified by numbers from 4 to 60 followed by the letter "d," which stands for "penny." For general framing and repair work, use common or box nails. Common nails are best suited to framing work where strength is important. Box nails are smaller in diameter than common nails, which makes them easier to drive and less likely to split wood. Use box nails for light work and thin materials. Most common and box nails have a cement or vinyl coating that improves their holding power.

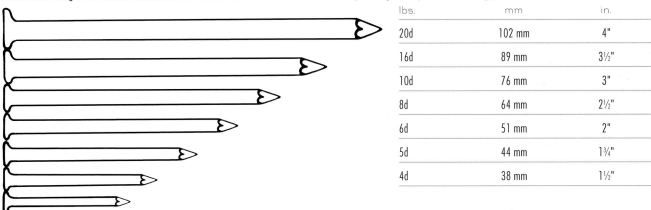

lbs.	mm	in.
20d	102 mm	4"
16d	89 mm	3½"
10d	76 mm	3"
8d	64 mm	2½"
6d	51 mm	2"
5d	44 mm	1¾"
4d	38 mm	1½"

Counterbore, Shank & Pilot Hole Diameters

Screw Size	Counterbore Diameter for Screw Head (in inches)	Clearance Hole for Screw Shank (in inches)	Pilot Hole Diameter	
			Hard Wood (in inches)	Soft Wood (in inches)
#1	.146 (⁹⁄₆₄)	⁵⁄₆₄	³⁄₆₄	¹⁄₃₂
#2	¼	³⁄₃₂	³⁄₆₄	¹⁄₃₂
#3	¼	⁷⁄₆₄	¹⁄₁₆	³⁄₆₄
#4	¼	⅛	¹⁄₁₆	³⁄₆₄
#5	¼	⅛	⁵⁄₆₄	¹⁄₁₆
#6	⁵⁄₁₆	⁹⁄₆₄	³⁄₃₂	⁵⁄₆₄
#7	⁵⁄₁₆	⁵⁄₃₂	³⁄₃₂	⁵⁄₆₄
#8	⅜	¹¹⁄₆₄	⅛	³⁄₃₂
#9	⅜	¹¹⁄₆₄	⅛	³⁄₃₂
#10	⅜	³⁄₁₆	⅛	⁷⁄₆₄
#11	½	³⁄₁₆	⁵⁄₃₂	⁹⁄₆₄
#12	½	⁷⁄₃₂	⁹⁄₆₄	⅛

Index